If you, or anyone you love, is tempted to think of Catholicism as anything but compelling and revolutionary, you need to read *Faith at the Edge*. This is an excellent book.

Brian Saint-Paul
Editor, InsideCatholic.com and *Crisis Magazine*

Faith at the Edge is a book for the new generation of Catholics. In this book, as on godspy.com, the Catholic faith isn't a weak old thing to be preserved and protected—it's a reality stronger and surer than all the modern messes we bring to it.

Tom Hoopes
Executive Editor, *National Catholic Register*

The post-modern conversion stories in this book demonstrate a great spiritual truth—that none of us is born a saint. But in God's plan, we're all born to become saints. There is an honesty here that is very rare in religious writing these days. These people have spied God, and glimpsed the mystery that lies at the heart of everything.

Scott Hahn
Author of *Reasons to Believe: How to Understand, Explain, and Defend the Catholic Faith*

This fascinating collection of essays by some of today's most provocative Catholic writers shows that the truly spiritual person looks at everything—including relationships, love, and sex—as invitations to experience God. *Faith at the Edge* helps to restore these topics—as well as a host of others—to the center of one's faith, and in doing so explains the Christian tradition for a new generation of believers.

James Martin, S.J.
Author of *My Life with the Saints*

This is a much needed book for the John Paul II generation of Catholics. There is a new and fresh spirit in the air of the Church, and Angelo Matera is making a substantial contribution to it.

Fr. Benedict J. Groeschel, C.F.R.
Author of *Arise from Darkness*

FAITH
AT THE
EDGE

A NEW GENERATION OF
CATHOLIC WRITERS
REFLECTS ON
LIFE, LOVE, SEX, AND
OTHER MYSTERIES

EDITED AND WITH AN INTRODUCTION BY **ANGELO MATERA**

ave maria press AmP Notre Dame, Indiana

"This is My Body" by Elizabeth Wirth originally appeared on *The Damaris Project* website (www.damarisproject.org).

"Like a Natural Woman" by Elizabeth Wirth originally appeared in *Re:Generation Quarterly*.

"Gay and Catholic" by David Morrison originally appeared in *Boston College Magazine*.

"The Sacrament of Matrimony" by Paula Huston originally appeared in *Signatures of Grace: Catholic Writers on the Sacraments* by Paula Huston and Thomas Grady, ed. (Plume 2001). Reprinted with permission of Plume. All rights reserved.

"A Young Father's Cry" and "Since Most Guys Do It" by Matthew Lickona, originally appeared in *San Diego News-Notes*.

"The Harsh and Dreadful Love of the Poor" by Marion Maendel originally appeared in the *Houston Catholic Worker*.

"Naked" by Austen Ivereigh originally appeared in *The Tablet*.

All other essays within this book originally appeared on the GodSpy website (www.godspy.com) or were written specifically for this book.

Founded in 1865, Ave Maria Press is a ministry of the Indiana Province of Holy Cross.

www.avemariapress.com

ISBN-10 1-59471-140-2 ISBN-13 978-1-59471-140-4

Cover and text design by Brian C. Conley.

Printed and bound in the United States of America.

Library of Congress Cataloging-in-Publication Data

Faith at the edge : a new generation of Catholic writers reflects on life, love, sex, and other mysteries / edited and with an Introduction by Angelo Matera.
        p. cm.
ISBN-13 : 978-1-59471-140-4 (pbk.)
ISBN-10 : 1-59471-140-2 (pbk.)
1. Catholic Church--Doctrines.   I. Matera, Angelo.
BX1751.3.F35 2008
230'.2--dc22

                                                    2007046580

CONTENTS

"FAITH HAS TO BE LIVED AGAIN AND AGAIN IN LIFE AND IN SUF- FERING, AS WELL AS IN THE GREAT JOYS THAT GOD SENDS US. IT IS NEVER SOMETHING THAT I CAN PUT IN MY POCKET LIKE A COIN."

–Pope Benedict XVI, "God and the World"

INTRODUCTION

Let me explain what *Faith at the Edge* means through a personal experience of mine.

Not long ago my teenage son had to write an essay comparing Christianity and Buddhism for his high school religion class. He knew I was curious about what he had written, so before handing the paper in, he let me look at it.

It was very good. As I read it, I grunted my approval. He clearly understood the major differences between the two religions. But a pained look came over my face as I read the conclusion. Here's the gist of what it said: "Christianity is about being a moral person and getting to heaven. Buddhism is about finding enlightenment and personal happiness."

"What's wrong, Dad?"

I looked up at him. "Do you really believe what you wrote at the end?"

He took the paper from me and glanced at the last paragraph.

"Sure."

It was a humbling moment. Here I was, a Catholic media expert who spent most of his time promoting the Church's "New Evangelization"—its fresh approach to preaching the gospel of Jesus Christ to a post-Christian world. Yet, I had failed to communicate the excitement of this message to my own son. I hadn't reached him with the truth that Christianity was about more than moral rules and the afterlife (as important as these are)—it was an adventure that was happening now, in this life, offering genuine wisdom and true happiness all the way to heaven. Where had I gone wrong?

Nowhere, I soon realized. Thanks to prayer and the spiritual counsel of close friends, I came to the obvious but difficult-to-accept conclusion that my son's perception of his religion was not at all unusual for a young person, and that what I wanted for him—a personal sense of the excitement of Christianity—was something he would have to learn for himself. It wasn't a truth I could spoon feed. He would have to discover it and test it—verify it, in the words of the Catholic theologian Luigi Giussani—and make it his own, in his life, in his time, through his own encounter with the living God.

That's what *Faith at the Edge* means. It's about the personal *experience* of Jesus Christ that comes from engaging both his Church and the world. It's about living the paradox of real Christianity—of being firmly rooted in religious tradition and authority, yet also open to what's new and provocative, what's unexpected and mysterious. It's about having rock-solid faith, but understanding that it's necessary to journey to the edge, into territory that isn't comfortable, to fulfill your destiny.

This is not easy. We're not used to connecting words like "tradition" and "authority" with words like "mysterious" and "unexpected." It seems contradictory. Of course, it doesn't help that every day in the media our cultural elites bombard us with the message that serious faith and being open to reality don't mix, that deeply religious people are just looking for simple answers to life's difficult questions. Our culture tells us that believing in religious certainty and moral absolutes is incompatible with critical thinking and personal fulfillment, and that doubt and skepticism—especially about the big questions of existence—are the true marks of a mature, well-developed personality. If you try to convince them otherwise, you're labeled intolerant, a fanatic—or a "fundamentalist."

The essays in this book are evidence that this view is wrong, that there are many religious believers who are attracted to the most challenging aspects of faith and of life. For these writers, simplistic answers aren't enough—they need to go deeper into mystery, into the darkness of faith, where certainty and the unknown merge into one paradoxical truth. They want to experience reality in all its terrible beauty, in the hope of coming face to face with God. That's what the writers of these essays have in common; that's what their stories are about.

Most of these works were published in the online magazine, GodSpy.com. GodSpy was launched five years ago specifically to reach Catholics (and seekers, too) who are looking for God at the edge, where the certainties of faith intersect with the shifting, unsettling realities of modern life. GodSpy's mission is to show—through compelling, personal writing—that being a committed, believing, orthodox Christian is compatible with being a thinking, feeling, culturally engaged person of the twenty-first century.

GodSpy is very much a product of my own personal journey, a trip that's been as surprising as it's been enlightening.

I became a Christian relatively late in life. While I grew up sort of Catholic, none of it stuck. My immigrant parents practiced an anti-clerical Catholicism that's not uncommon among southern Italians—they worshiped Jesus and venerated Mary and, of course, the saints, but they had little use for organized religion and priests. They couldn't care less when I told them, soon after I celebrated my first communion, that I wanted to drop out of religious education classes, which meant I wouldn't be "confirmed"—a sort of Catholic bar mitzvah that marks a teenager's coming of age in the Church. From that point on, as I grew up, I had no further contact with religion.

It was in college, at Columbia, that I first confronted the question of God, and encountered the great minds of Western civilization—Plato, Aristotle, Augustine, Aquinas, Descartes, Kant—as well as existentialists like Nietzsche, Kierkegaard, and Sartre. I became interested in questions of justice and truth, and the meaning of life. I read philosophical novels like Camus's *The Stranger*, and Hermann Hesse's *Siddhartha*, and discovered challenging filmmakers like Michelangelo Antonioni and Ingmar Bergman. I got involved in left-wing political movements, and came to admire the socialist and lapsed-Catholic Michael Harrington. I was deeply affected by the religious skepticism of these radical thinkers, but at the same time I took their social and ethical concerns—and spiritual struggles—very seriously.

All that came to a halt when college ended, and I began to think about how to earn money. It was the 1980s, and after a brief stint in journalism, I put my idealism aside and shifted to a career in the business end of magazine publishing. I spent that go-go decade living a typically secular, agnostic, hedonistic existence in Manhattan, chasing after empty pleasures, mostly money and women. But beneath the surface, a part of me was still searching for the meaning of life.

In that entire time, the Catholic Church—and the post-Vatican II turmoil that was roiling it—never once entered my consciousness (a state of mind I try to remember when I'm annoyed by people who are grossly ignorant of the Church). Only in my early thirties, after marriage and the birth of our first son, did I develop a serious interest in God, and first considered the possibility that organized religion might have the answers I was looking for.

I remember the specific moment that sparked my interest in the Catholic Church. It came from an unlikely source—a review of Pope John Paul II's encyclical *Veritatis Splendor* by gay writer Andrew Sullivan in *The New Republic*. I can still recall Sullivan's conflicted reaction to the pope's claim that it was possible to know absolute moral truth. As a gay man who couldn't accept the Church's teaching on homosexuality, Sullivan was repelled by what the pope wrote. But as a sincere Catholic he also found it difficult to resist the pope's "bracing" argument.

I'd always been a sucker for paradox, and I was fascinated by the idea that anyone as traditional and doctrinaire as a pope could be intellectually challenging. Given where I was in my spiritual journey—I had considered everything, but never the Catholic Church—I was hooked. I began devouring John Paul II's writings and other Catholic material, as well. I was on my way—I was turning Catholic.

But that wasn't all. While the pope was working on my intellect, my heart was being softened for Christ by the persistent witness of the Pentecostal doorman who stood watch over the Manhattan co-op apartment building my wife and I called home.

Jacob was a massive African-American ex-convict with a sonorous singing voice. He was also a scripture expert. He never seemed to miss an opportunity to launch into a lesson whenever I entered the building. If Jacob was on duty my wife and I knew we'd have to rush past him, straight to the elevators, or else endure at least fifteen minutes on the Old Testament.

But in the end, Jacob won. He wore me down. Thanks to his serene, rock-like, unquestionably spirit-filled personal witness—and his Bible lessons—I developed a personal relationship with Christ, for which I'll always be thankful.

The last influence on my conversion came from my wife Anna's direction. She had resumed attending Mass at our local parish, St. Stephen's, soon after our marriage, and had befriended several Carmelite religious sisters there. The simple faith of these holy women was impossible to ignore. Together with the pope and Jacob, they moved me along a slow path to the Catholic Church, and in 1996, at the age of thirty-seven, I was finally confirmed.

My newfound faith led me to some dramatic life decisions—all in a very conservative direction. Just before my second son was born, I moved my family out of decadent Manhattan to the family-friendly suburbs of Westchester. Then I sold my share of the growing marketing company I had co-founded, so I could work full-time in Catholic media. I left almost everything about my secular self behind, and adopted a new, intensely Catholic, somewhat reactionary, identity. (Politically, I was still to the left of Attila the Hun, but not by much). I was a newly minted true believer, and I started making every mistake a new convert could possibly make. I became very judgmental and Manichean (a fancy term for putting everyone and everything in the world into two columns—good and bad). I reduced Christianity to morality—avoiding sin—thereby totally misinterpreting what Pope John Paul II had written (as well as what Jacob had tried to communicate to me). Of course, I didn't notice this then. I was still feeling the rush of my conversion, still feeling that I had arrived home after a lifetime of wandering.

But eventually, I did start to realize that something was wrong. My harsh moralizing was causing problems within my family, and my "me and the Church against the world" stance was wearing me out, too. I began to yearn for a more joy-filled religious experience. My faith never faltered, but thankfully, it did start to evolve.

That evolution began when I started stumbling onto Catholic thinkers, mystics, and visionaries who were more dynamic and provocative—even subversive—than I ever expected. They led me to deeper insights into scripture and the early Fathers of the Church, as well as the lives and ideas of saints such as Francis, Dominic, Thomas Aquinas, Therese of Lisieux, and others. I was discovering aspects of the Church that had startling connections to the ideas that had inspired me in college, and the radical thinkers I used to love.

All of this was brought together for me in the provocative writings of theologians and writers who were part of the New Theology movement of the mid-twentieth century. This movement, also known by the name "Communio," had perhaps the greatest influence on the momentous Second Vatican Council—known as Vatican II—that was held in the early 1960s.

Contrary to popular perception, Vatican II wasn't about "updating" the Church. It was about reinvigorating it by going back to its radical origins so that it could more effectively preach the gospel to a secularized world. This return to the gospel and to genuine tradition was meant to purify the Church of subtle errors that had slipped in during the preceding centuries. These errors hadn't affected the dogmatic truths taught by the Church, but they did distort the style in which the gospel was communicated.

One important area where this occurred was in moral theology, as Dominican theologian Servais Pinckaers explained in his book, *The Sources of Christian Ethics*. Pinckaers showed that a shift within Christian morality after the Protestant Reformation, away from the desire for beatitude, or supreme happiness, to what he called an "ethic of obligation,"—making the obeying of moral laws an end in itself—had deformed the gospel message. This made it appear that the believer had to choose between being good and being happy. The answer, according to Pinckaers, was to return the requirements of the Commandments to their gospel context.

Pope Benedict made this theme the centerpiece of his first encyclical, *God Is Love*, where he addressed the various dimensions of eros (desire) and agape (sacrificial love), and argued that Christianity made it possible to reconcile these two aspects of love. The following words, culled from a homily given by Joseph Cardinal Ratzinger shortly before he became pope, capture the essence of the Christian message: "Christianity is not an intellectual system, a packet of dogmas, a moralism; Christianity is rather an encounter, a love story; it is an event. . . . Only Christ gives meaning to the whole of our life."

This is what Vatican II was about. And I was amazed to learn that my heroes—Karol Wojtyla (Pope John Paul II) and Joseph Ratzinger (Pope Benedict XVI)—had been two of the most influential thinkers at the Council.

My new perspective on the Church shook me to my core. I felt liberated. My church—all two thousand years of it—so often mocked and ridiculed in the media as archaic and obsolete, was turning out to be completely in sync with the search for meaning that defined my young adult years, and with concepts like mystery and creativity, freedom and desire. Salvation didn't require an escape from my humanity—it ran right through it. Pope John Paul II—the man whose writings first enticed me into the Church—said it like this:

> Man is the primary route that the Church must travel in fulfilling her mission: he is the primary and fundamental way for the Church, the way traced out by Christ himself, the way that leads invariably through the mystery of the Incarnation and the Redemption . . . man in all the truth of his life, in his conscience, in his continual inclination to sin and at the same time in his continual aspiration to truth, the good, the beautiful, justice and love.
>
> —*Redemptor Hominis*

From this vantage point I looked back at writers like Camus and Sartre, who accurately portrayed the excruciating loneliness and alienation of modern times, and saw their work from a new perspective, as description rather than prescription. They had confronted a new reality—the death of God in the world—without illusions, and asked the right question: How was man supposed to live with his newfound freedom? By taking the radical ideas of the modern era to their logical conclusions, they showed that life without God was absurd. And by so convincingly giving flesh, through their art, to what a world without God would be like, they unintentionally showed that only an uncompromising, radical Christianity could heal the existential wound that afflicted modern man. This is what Pope John Paul II meant in his "Letter to Artists":

> Even in situations where culture and the Church are far apart, art remains a kind of bridge to religious experience . . . Even when they explore the darkest depths of the soul or the most unsettling aspects of evil, artists give voice in a way to the universal desire for redemption.

Having discovered this new (yet ancient) "mystical" way of being a traditional Catholic, I could now see that my past and present were connected. I may have been lost, but my path had been marked by God. Passing through the spiritual desert of modern secular life, and directly experiencing a world where God was shunted aside, was, for me, a necessary prelude to a conscious, committed response to God's grace.

My new experience of faith thrilled me, but it also brought up an unsettling question—why wasn't the Church doing more to spread this message of Christian humanism to a world desperate for meaning? Sure, Pope John Paul II was talking about it all the time. But why weren't more people listening?

This brings me back to GodSpy and the reason it was launched. GodSpy's mission is to break through the misconceptions and prejudices that blind the gatekeepers of secular culture to the fact that Jesus Christ is the answer to the questions that haunt modern man.

In a post-modern world caught between the irrational certainties of religious fanatics and the dictatorship of "whatever" relativism, GodSpy offers an alternative—a Catholic vision that shows it's possible both to believe and think critically, to stand firm and remain open to reality, to live by moral absolutes and love unconditionally.

To reach the most skeptical, GodSpy emphasizes Catholic thinkers and writers who are most credible to secular audiences, showcasing nonfiction writing that fulfills what the acclaimed Catholic fiction writer Flannery O'Connor once said: "there is no reason why fixed dogma should fix anything that the writer sees in the world . . . dogma is an instrument for penetrating reality."

As the subtitle says, the essays in this anthology focus on "life, love, sex, and other mysteries." They cover topics, from dating, careers, marriage, childbirth, and parenting, to contentious issues like porn addiction, contraception, and same-sex attraction, to more mystical themes of identity, vocation, and interior transformation.

The subject matter is diverse, but what unites the writers of these essays is a singular vision: a paradoxical desire to live according to the firm doctrines of their church while at the same time freely expressing the truth of their experiences, and the judgment of their consciences. In other words, while as faithful Catholics these men and women are determined to obey their Church's controversial "hard" teachings concerning sex, divorce, contraception, serving the poor, loving the outcast, etc., as Catholic writers they believe they're called to tell the truth, to share the not-always-pretty details of their struggles, and to be candid about how hard it can be to live according to Church teachings.

They cannot write propaganda, not only because that would violate their personal integrity as Christians, but because if what the Church teaches is true—if these teachings are the genuine expression of what it means for people to love one another—this truth will only be compromised by any attempt to "suger-coat" it.

What sort of mysteries will you find within these essays?

Why "no pain, no gain" is okay for souls as well as bodies . . . what surrendering to God's will in marriage really means . . . why fertility is not a disease to be treated, but a wonderful gift . . . how marriage alone didn't cure an addiction to hardcore porn . . . why chastity is much more than just not having sex . . . what would lead a young father to make a deal with God over the inconvenient birth of his first child . . . how coming out gay was a necessary step in a woman's conversion to Catholicism . . . what it's like to grow up with the uneasy feeling that you're possessed by a demon . . . a childless woman's agonized confession about the real meaning of being open to life . . . what it's like to plunge into the freezing cold waters of Lourdes with hundreds of strangers . . . and much more.

As you read these essays, don't expect to be comfortable. Expect instead to experience a sort of cognitive dissonance, where you find yourself thinking: "Are faithful Catholics supposed to write like this? Are they supposed to be so . . . raw?"

The genuinely Catholic writer isn't afraid to be honest, and has no need to hide behind sentimentality. "We lost our innocence in the Fall," Flannery O'Connor writes,

> and our return to it is through the Redemption which was brought about by Christ's death and by our slow participation in it. Sentimentality is a skipping of this process in its concrete reality and an early arrival at a mock state of innocence.

Catholic tradition recognizes the paradox that it's through Adam's "happy fault"—his sin—that we've gained such a great Savior. Like the prodigal son, it's through the experience of our sinfulness—our nothingness without God—that we can learn to love. Only then can we return to the Father's house to claim the great inheritance reserved for his adopted sons and daughters.

While the Church's concern for souls is its highest priority, there is also something else at stake: Mankind itself is at risk as unrestrained science threatens to redefine life and what it means to be human. According to the Catholic philosopher Adrian J. Walker, a GodSpy contributor,

> If the Church has been concerned about sex and reproduction it is not because it is too 'hung up' to appreciate the glories of the sexual revolution, but because it has a mandate from Christ to safeguard the humanity of man, which threatens in our day to become the plaything of technology that is driven by powerful political and commercial interests.

The writers of these essays are witnesses to the narrow but necessary road the Church proposes for the times ahead. It's a difficult but rewarding path that integrates faith and freedom, and leads to genuine human liberation. Their stories show that it's possible to venture into spiritual borderlands without losing your way, and that faith at the edge is not only possible, it's the only way forward.

WHAT I DO NEXT PROBABLY WOULD
SHOCK A LOT OF PEOPLE, OR AT A
MINIMUM, STRIKE THEM AS ODD.

I SCOURGE
THE BODY ELECTRIC

by Brian Pessaro

The light on my alarm clock says 5:30 a.m. I rub my eyes with disbelief that I'm up at such a godforsaken hour. I stand in front of my dresser for what seems like eternity as I struggle against my desire to crawl back under the covers. In the end, I conquer . . . sort of.

In the darkness of our bedroom from beneath the comforter comes the voice of my half-asleep wife, "Don't even think about resetting your alarm. Go run." I groan and head to the bathroom to get changed. I pull on my sweatpants and sweatshirt and don my scarf, gloves, and wool cap. It's about 35 degrees on this cold December morning. Apparently, Tallahassee never got the memo that it's in Florida. Downstairs in the living room, I stretch my aching muscles. When I was younger, they would ache after my workout. Now they ache before I begin, as if they're anticipating the punishment I'm about to inflict on them.

The first mile of my run is always the slowest, but by the second I'm warming up and finding my groove. On the third mile I pass by the lake and shiver at the thought of being in water that cold. By the fourth mile I've increased my stride, and my kneecaps feel like they're about to explode. I see the final part of my route up ahead, a long hill. I feel tempted to walk, but I resist the urge and sprint with the last bit of energy I have. At the top, I slow to a trot and then to a walk and catch my breath. Despite the frosty weather, my back is drenched in sweat. As I climb the steps to my front porch, I give myself a pat on the back for working through the pain.

I'm sure many people, even non-joggers, could relate to what I've just described. When it comes to physical exercise, there is nothing particularly shocking about the old adage "no pain, no gain." What I do next, though, probably would shock a lot of people, or at a minimum, strike them as odd.

Back upstairs in the bathroom, I stand naked outside the shower door. Before entering, I make the Sign of the Cross and whisper a prayer. "Lord Jesus Christ, I offer up to you this cold shower in penance for my sins. I also offer it up as a prayer for . . ." I state the name of the person and intention for which I am praying, and then I open the door and step into the shower.

Because I'm still hot with sweat, the initial burst of water is a shock, but I get used to it. The water isn't so much cold as it is cool. I have it at about 70 percent cold.

After I finish washing, I put my hand on the handle bar that controls the temperature. I take a deep breath and crank it the rest of the way to 100 percent. There's about a two-second gap where the last of the warmer water clears out of the pipes, and then it hits me. I gasp as the water stings my flesh like a hundred ice-cold needles. This final part of my ritual doesn't last long. I say four prayers: an Our Father, a Hail Mary, a Glory Be, and finally, the prayer to St. Michael the Archangel.

Tempting though it is to rush through the words and be done with it, I force myself to say them at a normal pace. "St. Michael the Archangel, defend us in battle. Be our defense against the wickedness and snares of the devil. May God rebuke him we humbly pray. And do thou, O prince of the heavenly host, by the power of God, cast into hell Satan and all the evil spirits who prowl about the world seeking the ruin of souls." At the end of the prayer, I turn off the water and dry off to get ready for work.

Corporal mortification received a lot of press thanks to *The Da Vinci Code*. In the weeks leading up to the film's release, there was a cornucopia of news stories about Opus Dei, and in almost every one of them, the topic would eventually turn to corporal mortification. Inevitably the story would include a picture or a demonstration of the cilice, a spiked metal chain worn by the celibate members of Opus Dei around their upper thigh for two hours a day, and/or the "discipline," a cordlike whip used once a week against the back or buttocks while reciting a brief prayer. It became so commonplace that I started referring to that part of the report as the money shot.

Putting aside that *The Da Vinci Code's* portrayal of corporal mortification was as inaccurate as it was lurid, the fact that this practice shocks people says something about our priorities. In our society, it's considered perfectly normal to mortify our bodies so long as the reason is secular and the goal is physical. No one bats an eye at cosmetic plastic surgery, Botox, tattoos, and body piercing. Even physical fitness taken to extremes is looked upon as almost *de rigueur*. I'm all for staying in shape, but when I see joggers here in Florida sweating in ninety-five-degree heat during their run at lunch hour, I have to wonder: Are you *trying* to have a stroke?

None of these examples are controversial—titillating perhaps, but not controversial. But if you perform corporal mortification for religious reasons, to achieve some spiritual good, you're an oddball. To borrow an analogy from Boston College professor Peter Kreeft and give it a twist, if I were to announce at a cocktail party that I just got my tongue pierced, I would be surrounded by an eager crowd of spectators. But if I were to announce that each morning before work I take a cold shower as a religious ritual, I would soon be talking to myself.

So why do I practice corporal mortification? First, I do it to identify with the sufferings of Christ. By his passion, Jesus Christ redeemed the world for all eternity. But because he opened himself to all human suffering, including mine, I can share in his redemptive work. That is why I can say with St. Paul that "in my flesh I complete what is lacking in Christ's afflictions for the sake of his body, that is, the Church" (Col 1:24).

The second reason is to cultivate virtue. Most of us who grew up Catholic are familiar with the phrase "offer it up." As a child I was taught that in some mysterious way my suffering could be offered up to God as a prayer, and he would use it to help someone else. What I didn't realize was that he would also use my suffering to transform me.

This reality became clearer to me when I became a father. Recently, my daughter broke one of my neighbor's lawn ornaments. Although she's only three and a half, I thought it appropriate that there be punishment, or, if you like, penance—she lost her book and story privileges for a week. When I tucked her in the first night, she wailed because story time is her favorite activity. But the next night, she looked at me and said, "No books or story tonight, Daddy. I'll listen next time." In her own innocent way, she accepted her suffering and offered it back to me as a gift, and that gift transformed her into a more virtuous person.

If I, as my children's earthly father, use penance to build up goodness in them, how much more will our heavenly Father use penance to shape us into the sons and daughters he wants us to be for all eternity? That's what many people don't understand about corporal mortification. When I offer up my suffering from a cold shower, it's out of love, not fear. It's not an attempt to punish myself in order to dodge God's wrath. It's my way of asking him to transform me into the son he wants me to be.

The third reason why I practice corporal mortification is to be liberated from evil. Yes, my body is sacred, but it's also a rebel waging a civil war against my soul. Either I learn how to keep my passions and appetites under control, or they will control me. Too often when temptation comes, I find myself echoing the words of St. Paul: "I do not do what I want, but I do the very thing I hate" (Rom 7:15). These conflicts permeate all aspects of my daily life from the serious to the petty.

For example, my boss's secretary keeps a tin of chocolates on her desk for the staff. On several occasions, I've begun my day with the intent that I would fast from sweets for a particular prayer intention. But by three o'clock, I am distracted to the point of becoming a chocoholic version of Gollum and Smeagol from *The Lord of the Rings*—"Must have the precious!" Unlike the One Ring though, there's nothing evil about that piece of chocolate. It won't do me any good to go on a perilous journey to Pennsylvania and cast the One Chocolate into the fires of Mt. Hershey from whence it came.

That illustrates the fourth reason why I practice corporal mortification—to build perseverance. If I can't resist something as inconsequential as a piece of chocolate, how am I going to be able to resist real temptation when it comes my way? These little acts of self-denial build spiritual endurance in the same way my morning runs build physical endurance.

Finally, I practice corporal mortification to remind myself that this world isn't heaven. I live a very comfortable suburban life. Other than the occasional illness, pain and suffering are not part of my daily experience. Almost anything I want is at my fingertips—something as simple as a glass of filtered water with ice cubes or something as complex as music downloads from Napster. These are good things, but the danger of having all these creature comforts is that I'll start to get too attached to this world and its false idols—money, power, and lust. I'll fall into the trap of thinking this is my permanent home, when it's not. Corporal mortification rouses my senses and reminds me that in regard to this "earthly city," to use St. Augustine's term, I am but a sojourner in a strange land.

As morbidly fascinating as things like cilices, disciplines, and cold showers might be to the uninitiated, the truth is that exterior mortification is a piece of cake compared to interior mortification. To be completely honest, my body has gotten used to cold showers. It's the interior mortifications that I struggle with the most. Like my need to cultivate the virtue of patience and kill my selfish preoccupation with "my time," as if there really were such a thing. What makes this type of mortification so difficult is that when the occasions to practice it arise, they usually involve situations over which I have no control. Cold showers may be uncomfortable, but at least I'm the one controlling the temperature. What's more, they usually arise at moments when I'm at my weakest, such as when I'm hitting every single red light on my way home from work after I've already had a rough day. Or getting a phone call from someone just as I'm sitting down to finally read that book I've been dying to get to. Or having to rock my son at 3 a.m. because he's gasping and wheezing with croup, and there's nothing I can do to console him.

So do me a favor if you happen to read or watch *The Da Vinci Code*. When you get to the scene where Silas is flagellating himself to a bloody pulp at his "luxurious brownstone residence on the Rue La Bruyère," after committing the mortal sin of murder and planning to go out and do it again, think of this real-life scene instead. Think of a husband and father denying himself the pleasure of an extra hour's sleep in order to exercise and stay healthy for his wife and children. Think of this same man denying himself the pleasure of a warm shower in order to grow in the virtue of self-discipline. The cold water bouncing off his head and shoulders reminds him that sin causes pain, and he reflects on the pain he has caused others through his own lack of self-discipline. He carries that thought with him the rest of the day so that later that evening when his family needs him and he is tempted to be selfish with "his time," he'll remember the icy pain from that morning shower, and he will put their needs ahead of his own. When you can picture that, only then will you begin to understand corporal mortification.

AS I CRIED ALONG WITH MY NEW-
BORN SON, CHRISTOPHER, ONE
SLEEPLESS NIGHT, I REMEM-
BERED THE WORDS OF MY LORD
THE NIGHT BEFORE HE SACRI-
FICED HIMSELF FOR ME: "THIS IS
MY BODY, BROKEN FOR YOU."

THIS IS MY BODY

by Elizabeth Wirth

After a year of marriage, my husband and I decided to start actively trying to have a child. I wanted one so badly, I ached. We prayed and planned, charted and hoped. The day I surprised my husband with a positive pregnancy test, I couldn't remember being happier. I bought books on pregnancy, started taking vitamins, and looked forward to a blissful nine months.

Then I got sick. Really sick.

I had to eat Cheerios from the side of the bed in the morning before I even lifted my head off the pillow. Some days I could barely get up for exhaustion. I couldn't open the refrigerator or dishwasher without vomiting. Yes, I did go to work every day, but for three months I felt far worse than I ever had on a "sick day." Certainly, I knew that many women experienced far more difficult pregnancies and that my suffering was relatively minor. Still, it amazed me that women around the globe went through this routinely. I couldn't understand a paradigm in which this would be considered normal.

Of course, I loved the baby growing inside of me. I was preparing a home for him, avoiding alcohol, soft cheeses, and sushi, and choosing from *20,001 Baby Names* for him. I was supposed to be excited, glowing, and anticipatory. But I had never before felt so out of control.

Friends of mine, due the same month, giggled and exclaimed over their babies' first kicks. When I felt my baby's first kick, I felt squeamish and even a bit repulsed. I found it frightening rather than comforting. Here I was, growing somewhat resentful and increasingly disillusioned. I had chosen this. I had asked for this. I wanted this. Then why was it so foreign and creepy?

The fact was nothing in my life had prepared me for pregnancy. I simply had not been taught that my body was made for childbearing. Even as I write this, it feels like a betrayal of my gender. How can my body be "for" anything? I had learned that my body was my own, that no one could decide anything about it but me. Then what was going on?

For nine months, another person decided whether I kept my breakfast down or not. Another was stretching my skin, making room for himself. Another used me as an incubator, fed from me, and kicked my organs. As I looked and felt less and less like the person I had been, I cried out, "This is my body! What is happening to it?"

I prayed a lot during my pregnancy. I prayed for my baby's health. I prayed for him to have a good life. I prayed to feel better. I prayed not to throw up in any embarrassing places. I prayed that labor wouldn't hurt too much (I didn't say these were the noblest prayers). And I prayed for something to help this make sense.

My questioning only increased during Christopher's birth. I was fortunate in that my labor was "textbook," as if a textbook could encompass what it is like to give birth to a child. He was born after eleven hours of labor, no drugs (the anesthesiologist was "busy"), and the most energy I've ever expended on anything.

But as I was reveling in the beauty of my new baby, I marveled that my husband's body was exactly the same as it had been twenty-four hours before. I could barely recognize myself. My breasts were feeding troughs, and my stomach sagged in positions I didn't think possible.

All my modesty had been stripped away. By the time I delivered, I remember thinking that anyone could do just about anything to me and I would hardly notice.

With my body at the weakest point it had ever been, I embarked on the trial of actually raising my newborn. I wanted to spend the first night with him, to have him near me, to welcome him with love. But my body had reached its physical and emotional limits.

All I could do was cry. The nurses finally asked gently if I wanted them to take my baby out of the room so I could sleep. Sobbing, I agreed. It was my first night and already I felt that I had failed.

A few weeks later, as I cried along with Christopher one sleepless night, I remembered the words of my Lord the night before he sacrificed himself for me: "This is my body, broken for you."

He, too, spent a grueling, sleepless night of agony before the most difficult experience of his life. He, too, prayed before his suffering, asking his father for relief, wondering if there were any other way. He, too, lost his modesty, splayed naked before onlookers, laid bare while suffering and in pain. Jesus, God made flesh, was physically torn. He endured torment and exhaustion. His body had been broken, too. He understood what was happening to me.

The answer to the why—to what was happening to his body—was life. At the end of Jesus' sacrifice was life. Life for me. Life for all who would believe in him. Like me, he went through his agony with a name on his lips, the name of the one for whom this all made sense, for whom the pain and suffering were worthwhile. Like his suffering, my suffering was not meaningless.

The body that had endured so much to bring Christopher into the world now ached with joy. There in my arms lay a being that existed because of my love and my sacrifice. If my body had not been available and enduring, he would not have been there—and I could not imagine a world without him. Perhaps this paradigm was not "normal," but it was holy.

So I held Christopher close those sleepless nights when I thought I couldn't give one more ounce. When I thought I would collapse, I looked into his face and whispered, "This is my body—broken for you."

THE SACRED HEART STILL BURNS,
ON THE BOOKCASE NEXT TO THE
TELEVISION, HIS ALMOST LONELY
EYES WATCHING ME, WATCHING.

PORN AND THE SACRED HEART

by Patrick Still

I.

I was eleven years old when my best friend, Eddie, who was Italian and Catholic, told me he knew what a woman looked like, naked—from the front. Of course, I didn't believe him. I knew what breasts were, and sometimes I thought about them, but I never imagined there was anything below the waist that should interest me. I soon found out how wrong I was.

Eddie's father had stolen cable television service from the cable company through a small black box. All I remember about their Chicago bungalow is that the TV shared the living room with a portrait of an effeminate Jesus exposing his Sacred Heart. Though I wasn't Catholic, I was almost as interested in that alien, pasty

Jesus as I was in that criminal cable box, which beamed shiny images of human sex into my adolescent mind.

When his mom left the house, Eddie kept watch while I flipped to the "bad channel" and saw womanly glory for the first time. Now, a decade and half later, I can close my eyes and still see what I saw on that stolen porn channel. And the Sacred Heart still burns, on the bookcase next to the television, his almost lonely eyes watching me, watching.

II.

On the wall of our small dining room I've hung an icon of the Virgin with the child Jesus. It's only a paper icon cut from a diocesan newspaper and stuck to the wall with tape, unblessed and without votives. In the first months of our marriage, my wife and I would sometimes look at infant Jesus and his Mother when our conversation at dinner fell silent. Now, with an infant in the high chair next to us, there are no silent moments, and we have all but forgotten about the paper icon. Until our neighbors started doing it. And doing it. And then, after a twenty-minute respite, doing it again.

The new neighbors are young and unmarried, but they're in love; the daytime television kind of love, where their headboard smacks the wall of our dining room at least twice a day with the sort of percussion that leaves nothing to the imagination. As we sit with our eight-month-old daughter, suppressing the raunchier things we want to say, the sounds make pictures in my brain of sweaty men behind full-breasted women, grunting and heaving in the kind of absurd positions only practiced in porn. I shut their acts from my mind, and shake my head for being so susceptible to my adolescent intellect. But I still say to my wife, "It might be nice," and nod my head toward the wall with the Virgin icon, toward our neighbors' studio apartment. She chuckles grimly and says, "Are you sure you'd be up to that?"

It's been eight months since we last made love. Eight months since the birth of our daughter, and I'm not sure I'm up to anything. After countless discussions with our midwife and trips to the gynecologist, we still don't understand why my wife is not healing the way she should. "I've read that some women experience pain for a year after childbirth," she tells me, repeatedly. "Okay," I say darkly, "but they're at least having intercourse . . ." And then we sigh and look at each other, and then give each other shoulder rubs. Who knew sex in marriage could be this good?

Back in Eddie's living room, awash in sounds of tinny techno and fake moans of passion, we had no clue what real sex felt like, but we knew from watching porn that it was going to be awesome. Of course, none of the contrived plots involved anything like medical celibacy, and I never considered the possibility that I might live without sex as a married man. Between the age of eleven and my early twenties, I was too busy biding time until marriage, waiting to finally have-at-it with the woman of my dreams. Thanks to the thousands of sexual images I'd absorbed over a decade, I had a vast mental reservoir of masturbatory material to draw from, to make sure I never forgot how good an orgasm felt. And if that wasn't enough, my high school girlfriend let me do things to her, as long as we never crossed the line, as long as it wasn't intercourse. Being a good evangelical, I knew God wanted me to be a virgin on my wedding night.

III.

On our wedding night, there was something cathartic about being alone and naked with my wife without guilt. We were free in our sexual expression, unhindered by any mechanical or chemical contraceptives—the kind of sex good Catholics should have. Except it barely was sex in the full sense of the word. My bride's pain and our inexperience meant about forty minutes of fumbling and ten seconds of true union. All the fantasies I had about this moment, built up over years, collapsed into a heap, like tuxedo trousers on a hotel floor. Zealous, sheet-twisting coitus had been replaced by humble mystification. We looked at each other, unsure what had happened, and then tenderly laughed at ourselves in the candlelight before falling asleep in each other's arms. There was nothing reminiscent of pornography about it, and I was thankful.

Three months later, after a bit more practice, our contraception-free sex ended in conception. The morning after, I placed a thermometer in my wife's mouth and found it had risen by half of a degree. She had ovulated. I eloquently mumbled, "Oh shit," and we pored over our charts to see where exactly we went wrong. Our plans had "baby" only tentatively penciled in after two years of marriage. We soon realized that the biological signs that told us to make love in our midnight desire were the same ones telling us that ovulation was imminent.

I didn't fully accept the possibility of pregnancy until two days later, when I found myself at a small side altar to the Virgin of Guadalupe. I'd stopped into an empty church to pray on a whim—to clear my head. I was greeted by Our Lady, clothed in the native dress that revealed her belly was heavy with child. It was too early for my wife to take a pregnancy test, but as I knelt like Juan Diego and looked up into the face of Christ's mother, the painting seemed to smile at me in a way that guaranteed the pink strip would say yes. I grinned sheepishly back at the Virgin, wondering why I thought I could control my wife's fertility when I had barely controlled my own inclinations for the last ten years.

IV.

Nine months later, at 6:29 a.m. on a Wednesday, our daughter was born underwater into the capable hands of our nurse-midwife. With an elegant bloom of blood and tissue, her head opened the canal, her shoulders were extracted, and a wide-eyed infant was placed at the breast of my wife, who was crying with laughter.

That same small face, still wide-eyed under the water, was later the source of my own delight, as the deacon intoned, "In the name of the Father, the Son, and Holy

Spirit," and pulled my daughter headfirst through the baptismal font. This time it was I who pulled her to my chest as she emerged from the water. Holding her tiny, nude body, reborn through water and spirit, salvation suddenly became overwhelmingly sensual. I came forward to receive the body and blood of Christ with my newly baptized daughter in my arms.

For all of it—my Catholicism, our daughter, the baptism, and to some degree the celibacy—I can only blame my wife. And God. Years ago, when we had barely thought of marriage, she took me to a rural orphanage in Honduras, run by a toothless Franciscan. There, a humble tabernacle in a cement block chapel sent chills through my spine. I found a prayer of adoration to the Blessed Sacrament in an old book, next to a dusty kneeler. My callused evangelical heart was made raw by the possibility that the real presence of my Lord was silently waiting for me to notice him. I made sure I was alone, and read the words, holding their sweetness as long as I could. Quietly, I said, "I know you're in there, Jesus," and let my fingers ghost across the front of the tabernacle. Then I left before anyone saw my embarrassment for falling in love with a wafer locked up in a golden box.

V.

It's been eight months since I made love to my wife. Eight months since the birth of our daughter. Sometimes there are tears of frustration. Sometimes, I take secret pleasure in a sexual purity that I haven't known since the fifth grade. The stains of my sexual brokenness, that I thought had been cleansed by marriage, can't hide any longer behind the sloth of a satisfied husband in bed. I lay awake at night hoping that this celibacy is not permanent, but that the chastity—my own properly ordered sexuality—might be. This isn't purity based on unknowing, as if my mind could somehow regain the innocence of my prepubescent past. Rather, it's the purity that comes when you admit there are some corners of the devil's hell you still find overwhelmingly erotic, but still, once more, you decide to look away.

When I go to my priest seeking forgiveness, and ask him to absolve me for lusting in my heart, for sexual thoughts about a woman who is not my wife, I don't tell him that I'm living as a celibate. I don't want his sympathy. I just want a good communion on Sunday, where my eyes don't notice the comely shape of my neighbor's wife moments before I receive the body and blood of my Lord.

VI.

Now, in the background, the television is humming, casting shadows of exposed flesh somewhere deep in my subconscious. The shadows taunt me in dreams when I fall asleep with a rosary in my hands. Maybe they're afraid I might finally root them out. Yes, it's true; I can't yet turn them off completely. But whenever they take me back to Eddie's living room, I find my Lord is always there, with the flesh of his chest pulled back and his eyes aching for my attention. While women expose themselves on decade-old celluloid, and make love to men who are not their husbands, I busy myself studying the thorns that pierce the ventricles like veins, and the aorta on fire. I turn away from the shameful screen toward the nuptial passion of the Sacred Heart.

THE *ROLLING STONE* ARTICLE
FORCED ME TO A BRACING DECI-
SION: DID I CARE MORE ABOUT
READERS' APPROVAL AND MEN'S
ATTENTION OR THE APPROVAL OF
MY LORD?

CONFESSIONS OF AN UNDERCOVER VIRGIN

by Anna Broadway

I doubt any artist who moves to New York can avoid enduring a season of grim poverty. Mine began in May 2004, two years into my East Coast adventure (I moved there from Arizona), when my contract for a well-paying editing gig ended. It seemed like a good time to return to a languishing novel, collect unemployment for a few months, and figure out where my life was going. But before long I found more fertile territory to explore. I began blogging about my sex life (or lack thereof).

At first, my blog, Sexless in the City, was just a way to negotiate the tension between my desire to serve God by staying chaste—no matter what—and a sneaking suspicion he was gypping me out of life's good stuff by prolonging my search for a husband into my late twenties (patience has never been my strong suit). But from this conflict an original character was born: Anna Broadway (my *nom de plume*)—a Jesus freak whose romantic misadventures were almost exclusively drawn from dates with horny, freaked-by-Jesus men.

Anna's blogging was heavy on sarcastic self-deprecation and bawdy observations about dating and men . . . light on Christianity. Let's just say Anna—I—wasn't really "out" about my chastity or relationship with God. After all, I wanted to hold and expand my burgeoning audience, didn't I? Instead, I kept the spotlight on my stories; there were no lack of wacky, naughty adventures to retell. And while faithful readers could eventually guess why many men wandered through my life but never into my bed, I stayed coy about my status as a virgin.

Then came Jeff Sharlet—a religion journalist writing about the "new generation of young men and women" who were "embracing celibate life." He featured me prominently in his exposé. In a whirlwind two weeks—marathon holiday-weekend interview, photo shoot, and cover story in *Rolling Stone*—I was outed. Magazine cover lines labeled me part of a "new virgin army" in which I supplied "fire, brimstone, and brains." The article raised no little hoo-ha; within days page-views for Sexless had doubled, tripled, and even quadrupled. And with the readers came e-mails and comments about my chastity.

It was a shock. Before, I'd always been reluctant to disclose personal facts too quickly about my lack of a sex life. With men, it was a vulnerability best revealed on subsequent dates (if we got that far), or when I would eventually explain why I couldn't see them anymore. I'd keep my secret, use them for a few drinks, flirtation, and dates, then accept the inevitable parting of ways that followed.

But after the *Rolling Stone* story was published, and once I inked a book deal with Random House based on my blog, that wasn't an option any longer. There was no way to talk about my life and work without disclosing my "secret." And that clearly destroyed my chances of giving out my phone number or even exchanging much flirtation with any secular man I'd meet.

But it wasn't just that I couldn't get away with an undercover virgin's flirtation anymore; I had to reckon with who I was and what I claimed to stand for.

Though I'd always considered myself a girl who didn't play games with men, looking back I can see I was deceiving myself. Each time I dated a man who didn't share my faith, I wasn't playing straight with him.

While these guys knew I was a Christian, most didn't assume chastity was part of being religious. And while not all men were as crass as the one who told me, "Call me when you wanna f—k," none of the ones I dated were up for a girlfriend committed to pre-marital virginity (and not just in the "technical" sense). After I started *Sexless in the City*, I began to realize this, but I still wasn't ready to be honest.

But the *Rolling Stone* article forced me to a bracing decision: Did I care more about readers' approval and men's attention (both of which I thought depended on maintaining shock 'n' awe) or the approval of my Lord? Was I going to forego not just extramarital sex but the ways I'd been using men I knew I couldn't consider marrying?

I chose honesty—which is scary, but also liberating—and not as lonely as I'd thought.

A couple months ago, I ran into a bright young writer I'd met in the early days of *Sexless*. We had one of those great, electric conversations where two people who previously didn't have much to talk about suddenly find each other fascinating. But because he knew the stakes with me upfront, there was no question of him calling or somehow pursuing our modest chemistry. In that sense our interaction was more human for being stripped of the sizing-each-other-up that happens with a potential date or mate or lover. And it was more generous since we weren't thinking about how the other person could meet our needs. We were just taking each other for what we were.

I won't say I've completely recovered from using and manipulating men. But I've gotten much better at treating them more like brothers, rather than servants whose job it is to fawn over me.

This gets closer to the Christian sex ethic I've so long struggled to apply than did my old, rather legalistic abstinence. What *Rolling Stone* taught me was how much my dating—though somewhat true to the *practice* of chastity—disregarded its purpose and the whole spirit behind the "laws" I'd so long chafed against.

I CAME TO THE CHURCH'S TEACH-
ING ON CHASTITY BEFORE I
BECAME A CATHOLIC BECAUSE IT
MADE SO MUCH SENSE TO ME IN
LIGHT OF THE QUESTIONS I WAS
ASKING MYSELF ABOUT THE ESSEN-
TIAL NATURE OF LOVE.

GAY AND CATHOLIC

by David Morrison

In the tenth chapter of the Gospel of Mark, a young man runs up to Christ, kneels before him, and asks, "What must I do in order to inherit eternal life?" Jesus answers by enumerating what I call the party line: "Honor your father and your mother; keep the commandments." The young man replies, "Since my birth, I've done these things. What else do I need to do?" The evangelist records that Christ looked at him and loved him, and said, "Go, sell your possessions, give money to the poor, and come follow me." And the young man went away sorrowing, for he had many possessions. Like that man, every one of us, no matter what degree of same-sex attraction we might live with, no matter our temptations or weaknesses, asks Christ the same question, and every one of us has to hear his answer in our own lives.

I'm a convert to Catholicism, but I came to the Church's teaching on chastity before I became a Catholic because it made so much sense to me in light of the questions I was asking myself about the essential nature of love. The Church doesn't claim to know the origins of same-sex attraction, and—contrary to the thinking of a few bigoted Church members—she doesn't declare that the attraction is a sin. But she does call it an objective disorder, and she expects men and women living with same-sex attraction to live chastely, just as she expects all unmarried Christians to live chastely, which means no sex outside of marriage or before marriage. For that matter, married people, too, are expected to live chastely, which in their case means no contraception, along with sexual fidelity and commitment.

While all this is well known, people forget one part of the Church's teaching on chastity, which comes in the last paragraph on the topic in the catechism. There she says basically that, with the help of the sacraments and sacramental grace, and the help of friendship, men and women living with same-sex attraction can and should attain Christian perfection. The Catholic Church looks at me as an adult and says, "You might live with same-sex attraction, you might even define yourself as a homosexual, but we think that you can and will be a saint." And that, I believe, is head and shoulders above what anyone else says on the topic.

Some folks on the right tell me that because I live with a degree of same-sex attraction, I'm condemned to hell. Some people on the left say, "Poor thing, we consider you oppressed. You must expect to act on your inclinations; it's too much to ask you to live chastely." In a funny way, both sides are expressing much the same idea. On the one hand, the radical right tells me that I'm predestined to go to hell. On the other hand, the left tells me I'm predestined also—to act on my sexual inclinations. Neither is true, and the Catholic Church recognizes that.

I came to chastity because I loved my partner so much. I'm a veteran of a seventeen-year-long committed relationship with another man. It's a deep friendship, and it has been since almost the moment we met. It was sexually active for the first seven years, and then—after I became a Christian, after I began reflecting on what scripture and tradition had taught for two thousand years—I went to my partner and said, "I love you. Can we please stop having sex?"

That's what I said. What he heard me say was, "I don't love you anymore."

Thus started a year in which we disentangled the sexual aspects of our relationship from the rest of it. We came to understand that what we had together as friends—all the love, encouragement, honesty, affection, compassion, joy—we still had without the sex. That was ten years ago, and we've lived chastely ever since. Or to be more exact, only once after that date did we have sex. It was the night of my birthday, we'd both had a bit too much to drink, and we wound up having sex again. Afterward he realized what that had meant to me, and he resolved then that because he loved me and because I wanted to be chaste, he would help me. And he did.

What is genuine love? The supposition on the left is that if I can't have sex, my life must be loveless, lonely, and cold. And that's just not true. What I've come to understand is that erotic love is only one aspect of the love human beings experience, that we don't need to have sex to live a life that is joyful and committed and filled with friends and family. The question, then, is whether having sex is worth risking the kingdom of heaven.

This of course brings to mind the dialogue between Christ and the young man who asked what to do to attain eternal life. Jesus didn't tell him, "Go away and sell all your possessions," but simply, "Sell your possessions." Christ put his finger on the one thing in his life, the one thing in all our lives, that to give up, to make Christ the Lord in our lives, would be extremely difficult. Something for which we might go away sorrowing, or might turn our back and say, "Sorry, Christ, you're not for me." Jesus will honor our decision. He doesn't force himself on anybody. But he'll ask.

At bottom, the Church's teaching on homosexuality is a matter of discipleship. I turned forty this year, and all around me in my parish there are men and women about my age who don't self-define as gay or lesbian yet are no closer to being married than I am. And the Church expects them to live chastely as part of making Christ Lord in their lives. The issue is not what tempts us, then. The issue is how we live. Living chastely is hard, just like forgiving and asking others to forgive us, just like being charitable to folks who make us angry.

But following Christ is not impossibly hard. I have found, for example, that the growth of love in a chaste relationship can be every bit as deep as the love I experienced while I was having sex. And in the end, I don't believe that having homosexual sex is objectively loving because genuine love seeks what's best for the beloved—not merely what's convenient, not merely what feels good or reassuring or serves emotional needs, but what is truly best for the person we love. And I don't think homosexual sex is best for anybody. At the same time, there can be in friendship so much good and so much grace. God's love is like water. It finds a way.

So, my reaction to the Church's teaching on homosexuality is that we all should ask ourselves how willing we are to follow Christ and take him up on his offer. For it is a leap of faith. But it's been my experience, and the experience of a lot of people I know, that when we take the leap of faith, he's there to catch us, and he does catch us, and he'll catch you.

NEW ORLEANS MADE ME A CATHOLIC, OR AT LEAST THE KIND OF CATHOLIC I AM. IT ALWAYS SEEMED TO HAVE BODY AND SOUL—THE SACRED AND THE PROFANE LOCKED IN CONSTANT EMBRACE.

AFTER KATRINA

by Jessica Griffith

First, there is the thump of the road underneath the wheels of our Monte Carlo. Or rather, with each break in the pavement of I-10, two thumps: a heartbeat. I am small enough to fit in the space between the front seat and the back, to put my ear to the ground and listen to the bridge's metallic whine as we cross Lake Pontchartrain. I crawl around unrestrained, crane my neck into the rear windshield and look up and out at the expanse of blue sky, and then look for the line where sky becomes lake. I watch, as we ascend the high rise that crosses some port of New Orleans, the other cars stretching for miles behind, then turn quick at the apex to see the skyline emerge. This is my first memory of the city.

After the hurricane, I couldn't bear to read another "What It's Like to Miss New Orleans . . ." montage of the city's famed eccentricities. And I certainly don't want to write one. In fact, I've no right to claim the place. I grew up in a suburb on the north shore of Lake Pontchartrain. But all my earliest memories are of New Orleans—the twin spans of I-10 stretched out over the lake like two legs, carrying us to my grandparents, godparents, aunts, uncles, cousins. When I think back as far as I can, peeling back layer after layer to get at my first impressions of the world, I end up there, on I-10, on the same ramps that became home to thousands of refugees seeking higher ground after the levee broke. They always said it would. We thought it was just another urban legend.

This is the land where my mother was born and buried, and for me, it's sacred ground.

I cried as I watched the city disappear on network news, thinking that my daughter, still swimming safely in my womb at that moment, might never know the place that is literally the place of my dreams, the place that formed my imagination and my faith.

New Orleans made me a Catholic, or at least it made me the kind of Catholic I am. Its sins are famously great, for it is painfully human—has a city ever seemed so corporeal? Especially now, when we seem to be watching it die? But every place has sin. What distinguished New Orleans was that it seemed to have body and soul—the sacred and the profane locked in constant embrace. I think of an image I heard described just this morning in a news story—Archbishop Hughes holding the singer Charmaine Neville as she wept during the rescue efforts. "I'm convinced God is going to purify us through this," he said. Not too much, I hope.

In New Orleans, even the smallest actions are infused with a sacramental quality, and the traditions of the city—Carnival, king cakes, St. Joseph's Altars—are so wrapped up in the liturgical year and Catholic tradition that they constitute a lived catechesis. When I moved north as an adult, I worried that my faith had been improperly formed, that it was merely cultural, intuitive, not intellectual enough. Now, I wonder if growing up in New Orleans wasn't the best way to absorb the mysteries of faith. Baptized or not, when you live there, you take in Catholicism with the wet, heavy air you're forced to breathe. We were taught by example the importance of ritual, symbol, and paradox. We lived in a parish, not a county. I'd never heard the words secular culture. It's a beautiful thing—now that I'm a thousand miles away, when I get homesick, I go to church.

I don't pine for restaurants and jazz clubs or even Mardi Gras. To me, these are only the most obvious and superficial manifestations of the city's charm. All can and will be rebuilt, and anyway, I've never been to Galatoire's—hadn't even heard of it until I got my first job in Baton Rouge after college. Where I come from, we ate po' boys from gas stations—where you could also buy a rosary—and nightlife was bingo in the school cafeteria. What I miss most is the reliable sacredness of the everyday, now disrupted, indefinitely. Archbishop Hughes said that the Sunday after the storm might have been the first time since 1725 that no parish Masses were celebrated in the city.

Each time I have visited since moving away, it has felt more like a pilgrimage. I wander the streets of the city, splashing myself with holy water in St. Louis Cathedral and drinking beer at Molly's, like any good tourist, but I am motivated by a sense of obligation that I can only describe as religious—an urge to venerate, remember, practice. Not just for my sake, but so I can pass it down. At the end of the day, I drive across the twin spans of I-10.

My bridges, too, were destroyed by the storm surge, lost to the water like everything else. But I can still hear the thumping heartbeat of the road under my wheels, the continuous rhythmic pulse of the womb where I was fashioned.

WILL I BE SUCH A DIFFERENT PER-
SON WHEN GOD IS DONE WITH ME
THAT I'LL LOOK UPON TALLAHAS-
SEE WITH NEW EYES, AND LAUGH
AT THE FOOL I WAS FOR EVER
WANTING TO LEAVE?

MY TALLAHASSEE PURGATORY

by Brian Pessaro

I believe in purgatory. I've always expected that I would spend some time there after I died. I never knew though that, like heaven and hell, purgatory starts here and now, and I never realized that it looks exactly like Tallahassee. It's my own fault for getting here. Five years ago, I did something very bold . . . and very stupid. I told God, "I will go wherever you want me to go." I didn't realize he would actually take me up on the offer.

My purgatory began in June 2002 when my wife and I packed up our Corolla and moved across the country from San Diego to Florida. On my last day of work, a man in the elevator looked at my box of belongings and asked, "First day on the job?" I shook my head. "Last day. I'm moving to Florida." I still can see the incredulous look on his face and hear his one word question to me. "Why?"

I simply smiled back at him, my confidence unshaken. I knew the answer, or to put it better, I had felt the answer. It was a thump. As we drove east for the last time on Interstate 8, and I watched California fade in my rearview mirror, I laid the palm of my hand on my wife's pregnant tummy. A subtle thump reverberated against it. Three and a half years prior, we had made the move from Florida to California, in the same Corolla, just the two of us. Now we were headed back with an extra passenger. Florida was home. Florida was where family lived.

A lot had happened in those three and a half years besides getting pregnant with our first child. My outlook on life had changed. When we had moved to San Diego, it was all about me and what I wanted. I remember turning on the radio during our drive west and hearing a song that was popular at the time called "Lullaby." The melody and the lyrics are distinctly Californian, and they fueled my delusions of grandeur. Goodbye boring Sunshine State. California here we come.

San Diego certainly didn't disappoint. My job was in the heart of downtown, and for the first year, we lived in a high-rise apartment mere blocks from my office. Oftentimes after work, I would sneak up to the rooftop of our apartment building and bask with pride at the skyline of the city I now called home. This was the life I had dreamed of having. I had arrived.

For my wife, though, our first year in San Diego was more nightmare than dream. She was a middle-school teacher in Tampa, and my job relocation had required her to say goodbye to her students midway through the year. As she tearfully packed up her classroom belongings on her last day, I reassured her that San Diego would be a great move for us. What I really meant was that this would be a great move for me. Shortly after arriving in San Diego, my wife discovered that she was not certified to teach in California and that she would have to get a master's degree. She was devastated. No matter. I was having an excellent time.

A year later, we managed to buy a small, two-bedroom condo in an old streetcar suburb of town called University Heights. Given the ridiculous nature of San Diego real estate, this was no small feat. My wife enrolled in graduate studies at San Diego State University, and I continued to enjoy my chic, urban lifestyle. Though I could not walk to work anymore, I was still close enough to ride my bike, and my morning ride would take me through Balboa Park, the emerald jewel of downtown. On many of those mornings, the fog from the marine layer would cover the park like a soft blanket. As I rode past the museums on Del Prado Boulevard and biked over the Cabrillo Bridge, I would admire the Spanish colonial architecture, and I would say to myself, "I will never leave this." That pretty much summed up my whole attitude. It didn't matter to me that I yanked my wife out of her classroom in the middle of the school year. It didn't matter that I had accepted the job offer before discussing it with her, or, to make matters worse, that I accepted it for less salary than we agreed was sufficient. Moving out to San Diego was what I wanted, and now that I had it, no one was going to take it away from me.

And then something happened. My wife convinced me to go on a Marriage Encounter weekend with her.

After years of being absorbed in my own interests, my marriage had hit the rocks, and I thought divorce was inevitable. I am a child of divorced parents, and several of my family members have divorced also. I had always sworn to myself that this legacy would end with me. Yet when the dark night of the soul came to our marriage, I was the first one looking for the door. The irony was bitter. It was my wife that refused to go down without a fight.

As I sat in the conference room where the Marriage Encounter weekend was being held, I crossed my arms and listened skeptically to the presenting couples. I don't remember much from that weekend, but I do remember one specific statement that the husband on one of the presenting teams said. "Love is not a feeling. Love is a decision. You have to decide to love your wife each day." Now there is nothing spectacularly revealing about that statement. I am sure that I heard it several times before. But that simply shows how you never know what impact a simple word or two can have on someone. Because for some reason at that particular moment, in that particular setting, those words said by that particular person were like a hammer and a chisel to my hard outer shell. I had gone into marriage with the expectation that the romance I felt on my wedding day would always last by virtue of the fact that I was "in love." I had naïvely built my marriage on a feeling. Feelings are like the wind, though. They change. When our romance started to fizzle, I started searching for affirmation elsewhere, particularly in my career.

I don't remember anything else that was said that day. The presentations moved on to other subjects, but I was fixated on that one simple phrase, "love is a decision." I glanced over at my wife, who was sitting next to me and looking straight ahead at the presenters. Do I love this woman? I don't feel any love for her. Can I decide to love her? For a brief moment, I was terrified because I didn't know the answer. And then something occurred to me. If love is a decision, it follows that it is my decision. I can't control my feelings, but I can control my decisions. What had driven me to the despair of contemplating divorce was the perception that I had no control over the downward spiral of my marriage. But when this man described love as an act of the will, suddenly I wasn't looking for a parachute anymore. For the first time, I felt hope that I could pull our marriage out of its nosedive. As the presenting couple continued to speak and my wife continued to watch, I said to myself in silence, "I will love her."

I don't want to give the impression that everything has been smooth sailing since that day. The vices that I have spent a lifetime accumulating are now like squatters. They are quite content with the place they have found in my soul and are in no mood to be evicted. My worst squatter is pride, for that is what drove me to accept the job in San Diego without any consideration for my wife. Pride is different from his cousin, vanity. With vanity you're obsessed with what others think about you, but at least you care about something. With pride, though, you don't care about anyone but yourself. C. S. Lewis wrote that the problem with pride is that you spend so much time looking down on others that you never stop to look up.

Our Lady of the Rosary was a good antidote for that. OLR, as the parishioners call it, is a small Catholic church nestled in the heart of San Diego's Little Italy. It's one of those churches that makes you look up, literally. Above the altar, across the entire front wall, is a painting of the Crucifixion. At the back of the church, along the opposite wall, is the Final Judgment. High above on each side wall, the apostles and evangelists keep watch from their perches, and if you are bold enough to arch your head straight back and look up at the ceiling, you will be greeted by scenes from the various mysteries of the rosary. Only the hardest of hearts could gaze at the Crucifixion scene above the altar and not be pierced with sorrow. Only the proudest could look at the scene of the Final Judgment and not say, "I am dust."

After our Marriage Encounter weekend, I made a point of popping over to OLR during my lunch hour for the noon Mass. It was only several blocks from my office. It was on one of those occasions while sitting in the pew that I said to God, "OK, you've got my attention. I'll do what you want me to do. I'll go where you want me to go. Just show me." There was no theophany, no burning bush or pillar of fire. But over the course of the next year, things began to change. I started getting disenchanted with my job, and for the first time since moving out there, San Diego began losing some of its luster. I didn't know it at the time, but my wife had been saying a similar prayer herself. The change that happened for her was that she began having thoughts of starting a family, a subject that had always been a source of tension between us before then. The more we talked, the more the subject of Florida kept coming up, to the point where we decided it was time to move back.

And they lived happily ever after . . . Well, not quite, or at least not yet. As we drove east across the California desert, the lyrics to a familiar song played on the car radio.

> Welcome to the Hotel California . . .
> You can check out anytime you like,
> But you can never leave . . .

I didn't realize at the time how true those words were. I had thought that my struggle with selfishness was over, but in fact, it had just begun. After a brief year and a half in Orlando, we moved again, this time to Tallahassee to be closer to my wife's sister. Tallahassee. They say it's a nice place to raise a family. I'm convinced that's what people say about a town when they can't think of anything else nice to say about it. My wife and I are from large cities, me from Baltimore, and she from Cleveland. We like large cities. It's in our blood. So Tallahassee was never at the top of our list of cities to move to. Come to think of it, it wasn't even on the list. But when my job in Orlando began to keep me away from my family for weeks at a time, I knew something had to give. There's a famous line from *The Sound of Music*, "When the Lord closes a door, somewhere he opens a window." I'll give him credit. He certainly did a good job of closing doors when I was interviewing for a new job. And then one night, a window opened. My wife showed me a job listing in Tallahassee that she had found on the Internet. The application was due by midnight the next day.

It has been two and a half years since I hit the send button on that application. I wish I could report that our move to Tallahassee has been a blissful conclusion to our tumultuous journey, but I'd be lying. Mr. Don Henley was right. You can check out of the Hotel California, but you can never leave. On more than one occasion I have gone online and found aerial photographs of my old neighborhood in San Diego. I miss it. I want it back. What "it" is though is something I am still trying to figure out. Is the "it" I desire something base like my carefree lifestyle from before I was a father? Or is "it" something noble like the friends we made through Marriage Encounter and Our Lady of the Rosary? To be honest, it's both, and that is what makes my struggle so difficult. The chaff and the wheat are intermingled.

I believe Tallahassee is my purgatory, or at least part of it. It has a purifying quality to it as a small state capitol given my idolatrous obsession with having a big-city lifestyle. Though I hope I am less selfish than I was before, I would never delude myself into thinking I have been purged of all my selfishness. And therein lies the problem. Every last bit of it must die. The squatters have to be evicted. I believe God is using my time here in Tallahassee to do just that, and my purgatory will not end until he has finished his task. How quick or long it takes will depend on how much I choose to cooperate with him.

I trust that I will get through this. What I don't know is what comes afterward. When God gets done purifying me, will he release me from Tallahassee and allow me to move my family back to San Diego where my heart longs to go? Am I wrong for even having that desire? As I typed those last sentences, was God looking down on me and saying, "You still don't get it, do you?" Or will I be such a different person when God is done scrubbing me clean that I will look upon Tallahassee with new eyes and laugh at the fool I was for ever wanting to leave? I don't know. I can only repeat with hope the prayer of Thomas Merton,

> My Lord God, I have no idea where I am
> going. I do not see the road ahead of me. I
> cannot know for certain where it will end. .
> . . Therefore I will trust you always though
> I may seem to be lost . . . you will never
> leave me to face my perils alone.

IT WAS A GREAT SURPRISE TO ME TO
DISCOVER THAT THE CHURCH DOES
INDEED BAR THE GATES AT TIMES,
THAT JOINING THE CATHOLIC CHURCH
IS NOT NECESSARILY A MATTER OF
PERSONAL CHOICE.

THE SACRAMENT OF MATRIMONY

by Paula Huston

Many people don't realize that it is difficult to become a Catholic. I certainly never anticipated that my bid to enter the Church would become a vastly tangled affair that eventually required the annulment of my first marriage and a second wedding ceremony with Mike, who had already put in a good number of years as my legal spouse. In some vague, hazy way I assumed that Vatican II had ended "all that"—that the Church no longer much concerned itself with people's "private lives," those areas of our existence, specifically the bedroom, that we twenty-first-century individualists firmly believe to be "off limits."

My ignorance in this line was rather typical, I believe. People outside the context of lifetime Catholicism take note of the big events: the pope visiting Mexico, the disgruntlement that sometimes flares within the ranks over the not-yet—and maybe never—lifted requirement of priestly celibacy. Outsiders are willing to concede that Catholicism is a mysterious religion, full of odd, incomprehensible ritual, but they tend to interpret this mystery as simple confusion, sorted out and pared down later by the Protestant reformers. Others are less restrained in their criticisms. These folk may find religion itself rather harmless, more of a yawn than anything else, yet something about Catholic worship raises their ire; something about it morally offends and disgusts them. For such people, the rituals may call up the complex, at times downright nasty history of the Church-in-the-world, or its refusal to accommodate certain basic facts about how things are these days. They may symbolize an antiquated patriarchy (priests, bishops, cardinals, pope—all those men). However, such folk—and I used to be one of them—rarely conjecture about whether or not they could join if they wanted to. The Church is so enormous, after all; how can you explain a billion members without an open-door policy?

And so it was a great surprise to me to discover that the Church does indeed bar the gates at times, that joining the Catholic Church is not necessarily a matter of personal choice. "Surprise," actually, doesn't quite describe that discovery. The day I was told that I would have to drop out of the Rite of Christian Initiation for Adults (RCIA) program and seek an annulment before the Church could consider allowing me to participate in the sacraments as a full-fledged Catholic, I felt shock, pure and simple, in the sense of "the shock of the icy water took her breath away." Like many Americans of my generation, I'd never before run up against the kind of authority that places the integrity of institution over individual "rights." Along with shock, of course, came the simple human anger of being rejected.

As someone who had been AWOL from church for many years—not only AWOL, but utterly faithless—a serious reassessment on my side was now in order. The important thing, I thought, was God. I'd finally found him again; I didn't want to cloud that trembling, delicate new clarity on things. Did I really need corporate religion? Could I stick with this admittedly rocky new spiritual path without the inspiration of liturgical worship, sacrament, the warmth of a congregation shuffling in their pews around me? I knew that others had done it, at least for a while—religious geniuses like Paul, Francis, Teresa of Avila, George Fox. Yet their times of solitude all seemed to lead back to the same place: roles of leadership in the new, more vibrant version of the Church that grew up around them. Many of us, it seems, need the visceral unity of group worship, the shared symbols of "organized religion," the spiritual grit of religious discipline, the (at times) daunting authority of institution. I was afraid that if I tried to go it alone, I'd be tempted to take the path of least resistance, to create for myself a relationship with God that, more than anything, pleased and reassured me. Worse, that allowed me to remain aloof and critical.

My decision to proceed was not so much brave as it was desperate. I'd found something that spoke directly to the crying need within me and did so in ways that I could not command, surprising ways that kept me off balance, less apt to think I was running the show on my own. True, I could have gone to another church, an "easier church," as they put it in RCIA, "around the corner." But an easier church might not do the job, might not be able to tame this thing in me that needed taming.

MONTH AFTER MONTH, MY TEM-
PERATURE ROSE AND FELL AND MY
HORMONES MARCHED IN PERFECT
HARMONY. I HAD NO IDEA I WAS SO
BEAUTIFUL.

LIKE A NATURAL WOMAN

by Elizabeth Wirth

I always assumed I would go on the pill when I got married. The fact that I was a practicing and believing Catholic posed no contradiction. Certainly, I was aware of the Church's teaching about contraception, more or less—but I had never actually been taught it. I didn't know anyone who believed the doctrine, much less practiced it, and far from challenging my beliefs, no one had ever even brought up the subject. The only thing I knew was the statistic that approximately 90 percent of Catholics ignore the teaching. That, and the ubiquitous jokes: What do you call a woman on the rhythm method? Mommy.

Still, I'm the kind of person who hesitates before taking ibuprofen for a headache. Was I ready to take a drug every day, potentially for years, that would affect my entire reproductive system? Reading the list of potential side effects—depression, migraine headaches, loss of sex drive—and then meeting people who actually had experienced those side effects made me wonder even more. For the first time, I found myself open to what the Church might have to say about birth control. But when I started to question, I couldn't find anyone to give me a straight answer.

I decided that a good first step would be to ask a priest at the parish where we were to be married. Not being accustomed to discussing these issues with anyone, let alone a man whom I didn't really know, I nervously waited until the end of our meeting to bring up the subject. Finally, I asked if he could talk to me about the Church's teaching and give me any advice. He paused for several seconds and looked at me quizzically, as if he was trying to figure out if this was something I really wanted to know, or if I was only asking because I thought my Catholic mother could somehow hear. After about a minute, he mumbled, "Well, that's a complex question." I should talk to a doctor before doing anything rash, he said, because the method espoused by the Church was complicated and unreliable. I asked if he knew of any doctors—or anyone else, for that matter—with whom I could meet. As he ushered me out the door, he said he'd get some names for me. He never did. Was I really the first person ever to ask him about this?

Next came our pre-Cana wedding preparation, mandatory for marriage in the Catholic Church. I had been looking forward to the section on sexuality. I was prepared to disagree with the Church's unreasonable teaching, but at least I'd learn something about natural family planning (NFP)—the phrase I'd heard associated with Catholics and birth control.

To my surprise, the only mention of birth control was the chaplain making sure that we knew she was on "our side." She told a story of how a priest from a different parish had talked to her about the difficulty in getting brides not to use birth control. "Of course they don't want to!" she had told him. "It's a complicated process, involving mucus and charting. And it is for the woman's entire life!" She ended by telling us, "Yes, the Church says that it is a sin, and yes, you need to think about how you feel about that. But does that mean that you can't be Catholic and use birth control? Of course not. Does using birth control mean that you're still a good Catholic? Of course."

People wonder why Catholics have nagging guilt—well, I can tell you that being told, "Yes, it's a sin, but of course you should do it anyway" is profoundly confusing. It was their teaching, not my own, that I was trying to follow—but no one would teach me! I started to wonder if the 90 percent of those ignoring the teaching consisted of Catholics who actually had heard enough to disagree with the Church—or whether they had just gone through a process like this.

I considered abandoning my quest, but I still really didn't want to go on the pill. And I still had no idea what this mysterious "NFP" was. All I knew now was that it involved mucus. (Gross.) But that smacked enough of having some scientific basis that I decided to follow the priest's original advice and go to a doctor.

My first challenge was finding a gynecologist who would discuss the method with me. I was transferred several times on the telephone as the receptionists at my HMO tried to figure out what I was talking about. Finally, I got an appointment with the fertility specialist—since she was the one who used these methods to help women become pregnant, they seemed to be thinking, she could just reverse her usual advice for me.

To her credit, she tried to hide her surprise at my questions. But when she delicately asked, "Is this for religious reasons?" I felt my face redden with shame. I mumbled that I was Catholic, but wanted to know for other reasons too. At the word Catholic her face lit with a mixture of understanding and pity.

She did sit with me for over an hour and explained to me a method which involved charting my waking temperature each morning. Because of hormone changes around ovulation, that temperature rises several tenths of a percent at and after ovulation. She explained that I could chart my temperature, abstain from sexual intercourse starting approximately three days before the day I expected the temperature to rise based on previous cycles, and resume intercourse again after the temperature had risen. Her main point, though, was that the method was not reliable. "After all, kids are great, but you don't want to have too many, or too soon," she smiled, glancing at the picture of her two children on her desk.

Wasn't there something about mucus? I asked. Yes, she said, but that was just to support the temperature thing. "See how unreliable this is?" Her eyes smiled patiently. Finally, I asked, "So, if this is so unreliable, what are my other choices?" She lit up. Her presentation of birth control options ended with such a glowing recommendation of the pill that I could have sworn she owned stock in a drug company. Somewhat numb, I took the bus home, clutching the list of birth control methods in one hand and the basal temperature chart in the other. Was this truly my only option?

Somewhat desperate, I decided to do my own research. I logged on to Amazon.com and searched for a combination of "natural" and "birth control." My heart leapt when the site suggested dozens of books. So this thing existed? And people had written about it? And then, I found the community I didn't even realize I was longing for—peer reviews. One of the books had over thirty reviews from women who had read, used, and praised the method. One reviewer said that every woman should read this book to understand how her body worked—another claimed to have used the method with success for over nine years. Nine years? I'd been led to believe that I wouldn't last a week and a half.

Somewhat wary of what it would do to my future Amazon.com book suggestions, I ordered *Taking Charge of Your Fertility* by Toni Weschler. It was through Weschler's book that I finally learned the NFP method. At last, someone knew where I was coming from. Someone understood that I didn't want to put chemicals in my body or have a physical barrier in what was supposed to be a free and intimate experience. And someone explained the method to me, respecting me as an intelligent woman who had the capability to understand my own body. And as far as I could tell, she wasn't even Christian, let alone Catholic! She just cared about women and their reproductive choices.

NFP is not the justly ridiculed rhythm method, which involves vaguely guessing when the woman expects to ovulate and abstaining for a few days around day fourteen of her cycle. The full method involves charting the woman's waking temperature, changes in cervical fluid, and the position of the cervix. These fertility signals together indicate to the woman when her body is fertile. During that time she can either use barrier methods (this is known as the fertility awareness method) or abstain (NFP). So my gynecologist was right in telling me that her method was, indeed, unreliable, as she only taught me one of the three fertility signals.

Advocates of the method point to several benefits: increased communication between partners, lack of side effects from drugs, latex, or medications, and higher efficacy rates than barrier methods (NFP is over 98 percent effective when followed correctly). We found all these to be true, and my husband Karl and I agree that NFP is one of the best decisions we have made in our marriage.

But the turning point came for me as I watched, month after month, as my temperature rose and fell and my hormones marched in perfect harmony. I had no idea I was so beautiful. I found myself near tears one day looking at my chart and thinking, "Truly, I am fearfully and wonderfully made." My fertility is not a disease to be treated. It is a wonderful gift. I am a wonderful gift.

I'm not upset at those who didn't tell me about NFP. Some didn't know about it, and others really thought they were on my side. Perhaps people didn't want to mislead me and certainly didn't want to be blamed if I became pregnant unintentionally. But they made their suggestions knowing nothing about me.

Perhaps a child is a more welcome side effect to me than potentially aborting an embryo. Why did my doctor automatically assume that decision for me? NFP does involve discipline—making sure to monitor carefully and actually abstaining from sex during fertile times. But taking the pill involves discipline too, and only about a minute less time per day.

It is true that not all sexual partners are up for that kind of commitment—but my advisors didn't know my husband. NFP doesn't provide for the same consistent spontaneity of sex as the pill, but they didn't ask whether I think that sex and children ought to be that easily separated. In retrospect, I cannot believe that no one told me I could avoid the side effects of the pill by abstaining from sex a few days a month. And the fact that the method is completely free, but for the cost of a thermometer, makes the omission all the more alarming.

Perhaps the most surprising aspect of this experience was discovering how tied to the culture I truly am. As a Christian, I am at least somewhat used to being counter-cultural. The first sentence of this article is crazy enough to most people—what on earth do sex and marriage have to do with each other? But while my decision to refrain from sex until marriage had the wholehearted support of my Christian community, no one else I knew was struggling with the issue of birth control. I eventually ended up obeying Catholic teaching, largely inadvertently and for my own reasons. But as I have been obeying it, I am considering whether I have been wrong in assuming the neutrality of contraception—mostly because I have tasted the goodness of life and marriage without it. Had my previous position truly been informed by my faith, or was it just what the culture had taught me?

People continue to look at me funny when they find out I use NFP, and they still make fun of the Church's position. But I don't mind so much anymore. I've got my own version of the joke now: What do you call a woman practicing NFP? Free.

I WASN'T LOOKING FOR PORN. I
WOULD HAVE LIKED NOTHING BET-
TER THAN TO KEEP SILENT AND LET
THE MATTER PASS. BUT THIS WAS
A MAN I KNEW—THIS WAS RIGHT
IN FRONT OF ME.

SINCE MOST GUYS DO IT

by Matthew Lickona

While visiting a guy I know, I happened upon a magazine entitled *Submissive Girls*. The photo on the back cover showed a woman, bound and gagged, her naked breasts cinched by straps. I was not titillated. Though this was merely the extreme form of the objectification that occurs whenever a man lusts after a woman—whenever he makes her into something less than a person in his mind—it takes a soul more hardened than mine to enjoy that extreme.

Instead, I was dipped in misery because I knew I had to say something. Silence would have been a serious sin of omission. But how? How to tell another man that he is sinning, especially in matters sexual? How to espouse chastity without seeming judgmental, prudish, holier-than-thou?

Pop psychology has made nothing what it purports to be. Condemnation of sin indicates hypocrisy. Purity hints at repression. And evangelization is the work of busybodies whose own lives are either too dull or too messy for them to deal with. Willing the good of another person, seeking to obey God's will, is no longer within the realm of possible motives.

I am no hypocrite in this matter—I can condemn the sin and admit my own guilt in the same breath because I am a fallen man of imperfect will but less-imperfect intellect—at least when it comes to lust. Though I try to be pure, I don't think I'm repressed—I thoroughly enjoy sex with my wife. And I am not a busybody—I wasn't looking for porn. I would have liked nothing better than to keep silent and let the matter pass. In this, I lacked true charity, but I still knew my duty before God. To let a man persist in sin is to let fester a wound in the body of Christ. I may not be called to preach to strangers, but this was a man I knew—this was right in front of me.

I wanted to keep silent because I knew the guy didn't think lust was a big deal, and I felt foolish making an issue of it. Lust has become recreational, an accepted part of manhood, rather than a temptation against which men must struggle. (I'm talking about men because it's what I know.) Strip clubs, porno movies, regular movies with explicit sex scenes, billboards, television—hell, just looking at women on the street, displaying their bodies in ways that leave ever less to the imagination. It's all commonplace—the culture aims for the crotch. This particular serpent has been around for a long time, but now it basks in the sun instead of skulking in the shadows.

It gets in the blood. There is something in my soul that associates sexual purity with stilted priggishness, instead of a manly struggle against the world, the flesh, and the devil. Every now and then, usually after I've been making a conscious effort not to notice scantily clad women on TV, on the street, in church, I hear a little voice saying, "It's not that big a deal. By straining to avoid it, you make it a greater temptation than it really is."

This voice echoes in the silence that emanates from the pulpit on this matter. I don't think I've ever heard a sermon addressing lust head-on, though it is a common and deadly sin. Not just adultery and premarital sex, though they are important and rarely mentioned, but the interior motion of the will: an illicit desire, contrary to the love of God and neighbor, the adultery in the heart that Christ warned against. The silence makes evangelization more difficult as well. If the priest says nothing, what business do I have telling a man that he is sinning?

And sometimes, when the priest does speak, he uses the culture's voice. Once, while confessing at a parish in San Diego, I was told by the priest that viewing a certain amount of pornography was normal and natural. If it got to be excessive, well, then I should seek counseling. If by "normal and natural," he meant that most guys do it, and that our nature (fallen) tends toward it, fine. But I think he meant that since most guys do it, it wasn't that big a deal. Since when can a man sin in moderation?

I eventually wrote the guy with the magazine a letter. I quoted the Catechism, which explicitly condemns pornography as a grave offense, since it removes sex from its proper context. I wrote about how lust drives a wedge between spouses, including lust after a stranger in a photograph. Turning your sexual appetite away from its proper object—your wife—is a form of infidelity. I shared my own struggles, the prayers I say when tempted, the pardon and strength that come from confession. He never responded, and I haven't asked him about it. I still feel foolish; I still stumble in my attempt to witness.

IT WAS TEMPTING TO MAKE AN
ICON OF MYSELF: INTELLIGENT
YOUNG WOMAN GIVES UP PROMIS-
ING CAREER PATH TO SHINE AS
MOTHER OF SIX. BUT LESS AND
LESS CAN I SEE WHO I AM, WHAT
IT'S ALL ABOUT, HOW IT WILL END.

MOTHERHOOD AS VOCATION

by Lisa Lickona

In high school I had a friend named Mara, the leader of our little clique of intellectuals—a future salutatorian, someone I looked up to. One day she prophesied that our friend Stephanie would never get married, but would have many children. "And Lisa," she added, looking at me, "I can't imagine Lisa without a husband, but I can't imagine her with children." I don't know where Mara and Stephanie are right now, but as for me, I'm at home teaching my six children.

How did I get here? For years Mara's oracle stuck with me—because it seemed so true. From the time I was a child I fancied myself a career woman. I don't ever remember playing with dolls, but I remember creating stores and selling my wares to the neighborhood children. I organized my own library and created my own imaginary designer clothing line. As I grew older, the career plans shifted—from designer to lawyer to linguist to teacher to theologian—but I never imagined myself a mother. Even when I fell in love and became engaged in college, I hardly thought about children. I clung to a grand vision of myself as a scholar or author or teacher, a woman who marched into the world and took charge, a woman who did important things and "made a difference."

When I was in eighth grade I cast myself as Joan of Arc in a play that a classmate and I co-wrote and performed. I loved Joan with her visions and her cropped hair and her armor. I loved her blend of virginal purity and masculine power. As I entered graduate school to study theology, it was probably the figure of Joan that most illuminated my view of myself. It probably wasn't until I saw motherhood as a form of feminine crusade that I began to be able to see myself as a mother.

It was also in graduate school that I encountered the writings of Pope John Paul II, who proclaimed a "new feminism." I pored over the texts, intrigued. In his writings, John Paul praised women who worked at every kind of job, recognizing them as agents of change in an inhuman world. But what was most important was the way women entered the world. Their "unique genius," John Paul insisted, was their capacity to personalize everything, to be present as humanizers. After all, wasn't it a woman whom God had chosen to radiate the very face of God to the newborn child, to awaken the child to the wonder of love, the reality of Being? For a woman to be present in this way to another human being, to let herself become a mother and then to carry that mothering sensibility into the world—the sense of the ineffable value of each person, no matter how small or broken—that, it seemed to me, was a crusade, and it drew me into the mission of motherhood.

The reality of this hit me when Steven and Anna Maria next door had a baby boy. Theirs was the first baby in the little Catholic ghetto that my husband Mark and I had settled into, a suburban Maryland apartment complex that housed graduate students from Catholic University. After three months of parenting, Steven and Anna Maria needed a night out. Mark and I volunteered to babysit. That night, while I held the baby, something inside of me awoke and said, "Yes." We conceived our daughter Monica only a few months later. Kateri followed two years after that.

I loved my girls. I spent all day with them, and then at night I read for hours to finish my degree. Mark and I had no money then, and we've never really had what I would consider an adequate income for a large family. We've gotten a lot of help from our family and I've slowly mastered the art of frugality. My father grew up during the Depression, and with him always in mind I can't help but think about money. I do a poor job of trusting God to send our daily bread, preferring to bake it myself. For me to end up with six children something—or someone— had to intervene. And she did.

I've always believed in and revered the saints, but only once have I felt that a saint truly entered my life from the outside, that a saint was not simply a person for whom I ought to feel affection, but one who felt affection for me. It was in 1997, after watching the Alain Cavalier film *Therese* that St. Therese of Lisieux—the Little

Flower—entered my life. For a while I ate, drank, and slept Therese. I read her autobiography, her letters, the accounts of her sisters. I talked to her. I asked for help.

Therese's short life—most of it spent in a cloister— was a complete surrender to the will of God. What she lived here was a grand and harrowing mission: to love God without restraint even in the darkest moments, to subject herself to the consuming fire of divine love. This was someone I wanted to imitate, a big sister in the spiritual life.

But one night, as I reread *The Story of a Soul,* I was caught up short. Suddenly, the distance between us seemed vast, the differences profound. How could I, a twenty-first-century married woman mired in the myriad duties of my state in life, attain the mystical heights that Therese, a nineteenth-century cloistered Carmelite, could? My life seemed scattered and mundane by comparison—daily wading through laundry and diapers, combing the paper for coupons, driving the children to dance classes, chatting up the other moms in the hall. There were no grand penances, no overarching monastic rule. I wasn't even all that good at getting up at the same time every day. It seemed to me that I could never, in my lowly married womanhood, attain the purity and austerity of Therese's Carmelite life.

Then I remembered that it wasn't the externals that defined Therese—it was the love. "I will be love at the heart of the Church," she had declared. I asked myself, "How can I stretch beyond myself right here, right now, in these circumstances?" The answer seemed clear: have children. Have more than I thought I could. Be love at the heart of my family. Not long after that, Maximilian was born. Two years later, our twins, Mary Rose and Lillian Joan. And then, two and a half years ago, our little Clare.

So now I have my "mission" and my "rule"—marked out by the demands of these six young souls. But what had once seemed like an end in itself now seems to be only a beginning.

In a pious little comic book that sits on my children's shelf, there's a picture of Joan of Arc in prison, bent and broken, her head with its roughly cropped hair resting in her delicate hands. All crusades, if they're of God, end like this, it seems. When we think we've given everything we ought to give, God takes our heart from our chest and puts it in the winepress to squeeze out a few more drops. So it was with Therese, too. Eighteen months before her death, the girl who seemed to see everything around her as though illuminated by her own private heavenly ray suddenly found herself in the dark, and the very existence of heaven was thrown into doubt.

For me, there have been no dramatic dark nights, but certainly a gray kind of haze. It was tempting to make an icon of myself: intelligent young woman gives up promising career path to shine as mother of six. But less and less can I see who I am, what it's all about, how it will end. Everyone knows that everything a mother does is a little sacrifice—all those bits of daily grind that have to be done to keep a household moving. But to accomplish these sacrifices in a world that's at best unappreciative, or at worst deeply hostile to motherhood—to keep everything balanced and joyous, stimulating and safe, to be kind to my children, to teach them to love what's great and beautiful—every bit of me shrinks before the task. Every fiber of my being is shown up to be the flabby, underused spiritual muscle that it is.

If there's a sign of our generation, it's the "breakdown of the family." Like so many of my peers, I come from a broken-down family. As my children have grown, and I've grown into being a mother, I've been more and more conscious of the wound in my heart that is my parents' divorce. It's the biggest challenge to my faith. It's the fear that haunts my marriage. Can love last forever? Can it withstand the wear and tear of life? And just so, my motherhood is threatened. How can I be love at the heart of the family when I'm not sure if love exists, when a secret voice whispers inside of me, "What's it all for?"

So often, it's with this voice that I speak to my children. I hear myself accusing with the voice of the Accuser, tearing down instead of building up. When I step back and take a look at myself, I'm shocked at the abyss that opens up between who I am supposed to be and what I am. It's a gigantic hole that threatens to swallow us all up.

Not long ago, I went through Monica and Kateri's room on the way to the attic. Ten-year-old Kateri's dresser is a typical little girl's collection of dolls and memorabilia. As I breezed past, I was caught up short. Taped up in the middle of the mirror was a note that read, "God loves me and the whole world," written large in black marker.

I marveled. How did she come to know this? I could clearly see how I've failed to be present to my children, to radiate God's love to them. But in that moment, I could just as clearly see that what is lacking in me is being made up in the motherhood of the Church.

Some months before I had a darker-than-gray moment when I realized just how sporadic and uneven my prayer was. I knew the cause: that old failure of faith in the love of God that sapped my will and wrecked my daily resolve. But, miraculously, an answer seemed to come: follow the rhythms of the family. A memory came to me from Catholic school of the daily prayers that sent us off to class, to the lunchroom, to the buses. So, I resolved to pray faithfully with the children—a morning offering before breakfast, the Angelus at lunch, the Salve Regina before bed. It wasn't anything really. But maybe it was something. And, in that later moment, standing before the mirror in the girls' room, there seemed to be a little confirmation—yes, it is something.

> The angel of the Lord declared unto Mary
> —And she conceived by the Holy Spirit.

As I get older the idealism of my younger days seems concentrated in this scene between the angel and the Virgin who will become a mother. It's clear to me now that this is the icon that I'm seeking, an image of a Mother who can carry my motherhood, who can bring it to fulfillment. So, there it is, my grand work: bringing my children to Mary and the angels and the saints and hoping that they'll bring these little souls to the throne of God. And hoping, in the process, that I'll get there, too.

I WAS TWENTY-THREE. I WAS TER-
RIFIED. SO I OFFERED GOD AN
ABSURD DEAL. IF I SURRENDERED
MY WILL AND ACCEPTED THIS
CHILD, MAYBE HE WOULD THEN
TAKE IT AWAY.

A YOUNG FATHER'S CRY

by Matthew Lickona

I was a virgin when I married, an achievement best credited to grace, formation, and the avoidance of the occasion. I remained a virgin for the first four days of my marriage, an achievement best credited to a strong desire not to conceive a child. To a young Catholic trying to toe the party line, it can seem a cruel joke—you manage to save sex for the marriage bed, only to arrive and find the event cancelled due to ovulation. Contraception is forbidden, as are the standard sexual substitutes of fellatio and masturbation. If you don't want to conceive, you're left with natural family planning—monitoring the woman's temperature and cervical mucus for signs of fertility and abstaining from sex accordingly. NFP works—my brother and his wife waited two and a half years to conceive their first—and besides submitting to authority, I concur with the Church's reasoning in these matters. But that was cold comfort during those first four nights.

We could have just gone ahead and conceived. Children are one of the two great ends of marriage, and we promised during our wedding Mass to accept them as gifts from the Lord. The Church teaches that even licit means of avoiding conception should be employed only for just reasons. What constitutes a "just" reason is a matter of prudential judgment. Here was mine: I wanted a year to rejoice over my bride, to develop the ease of living together and to solidify the marital bonds between us.

I did okay for three months. By "okay," I mean I merely pestered my poor bride incessantly for sex during our periods of abstention, without quite breaking down and saying, "Bring on the kids; I want lovin'!" I wanted It, but I didn't want Them, and my wife was forced again and again to confront me with this fact. My halfhearted demands made her feel like I was accusing her of holding out, like it was somehow her fault for being fertile. Hardly loving; hardly the spirit of natural family planning. But I didn't reform. I made up songs.

To the tune of *The Twelve Days of Christmas* I wrote:

> On the fifth day of Dry Times my true love
> said to me,
> At least a week
> The chart says I'm fertile
> My fluid's stretchy
> Let's hold hands
> And you can't have any nookie!

It got to the point where I scratched "nookie" in the leather of my shoe with my fingernail, an event my wife has never forgotten. During that third month, we got lazy about charting the signs, and a slight milkiness in her mucus was all the sign I needed that we were good to go. Needless to say, we conceived.

My wife got a yeast infection, then missed her period. We went to a women's health clinic. The nurse chuckled as she told my wife she was pregnant—of course! My wife came out and told me the news with an air of quiet excitement. I was, ridiculously, stunned. While she paid the bill, I left the clinic's lobby and stepped out onto a concrete balcony. I actually stared at the sky. I knew that I would eventually become a father. I did not want to become a father yet. I was twenty-three; I was terrified. I offered God an absurd deal (almost as absurd as offering God a deal at all): If I surrendered my will and accepted this child, perhaps he would then take it away. Perhaps my wife would miscarry. Perhaps this could all be just a test. I held on to that notion for maybe three days before I did break down and accepted that my wife was pregnant, and was likely to stay that way until the birth of our first child.

Opponents of abortion are fond of this quote from Mother Teresa: "It is a poverty that a child must die so that you may live as you wish." Procuring an abortion never entered my mind. Instead, I asked for one from God. I asked him to terminate the pregnancy. God would not be culpable—as the author of life, he may take life when he wishes. And I would have had no active part in the abortion—except that I would have prayed for it. My first-born son is six now; and seeing him in all his manifest personhood makes my reaction seem monstrous. I see the truth in Mother Teresa's claim: what a tremendous poverty to have wished that he go away and leave me in peace.

THERE ARE TWO TYPES OF GOOD
CATHOLIC WOMEN, AND THEN
THERE IS ME. AT LEAST THAT'S THE
WAY IT FEELS SOMETIMES.

OPEN TO LIFE

by Rebecca Robinson

There are two basic types of good Catholic women. There are the married ones with rows of children in graduated sizes, the ones I call "bunnies with minibuses"— affectionately or snidely, depending on my mood. The other type is an avowed religious, locked away in a convent in a more desolate part of your home state, making cheese to sell while maintaining a constant state of ecstasy. There are two types of good Catholic women, and then there is me. At least that's the way it feels sometimes.

It feels that way after coming home from yet another Mass at which three new babies were baptized and another cluster of pregnant women and their husbands gathered in the Lady Chapel for another blessing of expectant parents.

I believe in the goodness of families. I believe in being open to life. I have no children.

Or you could say that there are two kinds of Catholic women, the Good and the Dissenting. The Goodies look radiant under their lace chapel veils, smiling broodingly over the mounded belly of a fifth pregnancy as they herd their four external children into a pew at daily Mass. The Dissenters don't go to my parish, but I read about them, angry and restless and wearing pants, raising their voices in favor of birth control and a married female priesthood. Then there is me, resentfully orthodox, hanging onto the Church by the hem of her bedraggled skirt. At least it feels that way after reading, in my diocesan newspaper, a column of letters to the editor calling for abortion rights, after listening to yet another middle-aged mother talk about how we need to have more Catholic babies so we don't get bred out of existence by Muslims.

Or to look at this another way: There are the mothers of the Catholic tradition that I adopted, and then there are the Protestant, reformed wives among whom I grew up. The Catholic mothers that I know give birth with indefatigable regularity; they stop at nothing to produce souls for God (and, they hope, a future priest or two). They live in a kind of warm bath of good-natured untidiness, straggling into daily Mass to fill up a pew with the fruits of their unstoppable wombs. The Reformed wives I knew as a child, however, reproduced parsimoniously, carefully, as if they were haggling to get the best bargain. Children were a blessing, but a troublesome one; these good ladies and their male counterparts frowned on unfettered fertility, perhaps from a Calvinist love of order and control. Then there is me, wanting desperately to side with the overflowing Catholic minibuses, especially when a Reformed matron with perfect hair tells me how smart I am to wait before having children, and I long to tell her in no uncertain terms how glibly she has misinterpreted my childlessness.

I will tell you something about NFP—natural family planning to the uninitiated. It is scientific, it is healthy, it is moral, and yes, it works. If you go to the NFP classes run by your local bunny you may be tempted to believe, watching her hoist her seventh baby, that it doesn't work; hearing her talk about mucus, you may hope it doesn't. But it does. I have used it long enough by now that I can tick off the phases of my monthly cycle the way a mother ticks off the little piggies on her baby's toes, and I remain nonpregnant.

I will tell you something else, something the books I've read on the subject of Catholic sex don't mention: You are not guaranteed a mere seven days of abstinence each cycle. That is the norm, that sweet, neat week of continence that makes you feel so virtuous, but if you have a husband who leaves town a great deal, the sweetness and neatness become less apparent, as does the feeling of virtue. And supposing the roof of your world caves in and your tiny scraps of security go screaming into the wind as a tornado of marital and financial woe knocks you off your feet, forcing you into the category of those who have (to use the language of the Catechism and various encyclicals) just reasons to postpone pregnancy . . . at least for another month? Two months. Six. And then the stress of it kicks your system in the ass and your body begins giving you mixed fertility signs day after day, week after week, and the next thing you know you realize you have been abstinent for a month. I guess this isn't in the Catholic sex manuals because books preaching the beauty of married sexual love probably would rather avoid the issue of its occasional lengthy absence. This, I realize, is not a big selling point for NFP, and it's the sort of thing that feeds the rampant idea that the Church is a killjoy. If you listen to people like me, you might start to think that Catholics don't have sex at all. Then you read the papers and amend that thought to: Catholics don't have sex unless they are pedophilic priests, lesbian nuns, and bunnies with minibuses.

I'm tempted to tell anyone who might be reading this not to listen to me, a half-bad Catholic hanging on to the Church by the skin of her teeth through life's upheavals and a sense of isolation that at times feels so thick I could almost hang myself from it. But the fact is that you *should* listen to me because I can tell you something about what it means to be a Catholic that you will probably never hear from a priest or an apologist.

Let me tell you what happens when you find yourself heading into a new month and you have lived with your spouse as brother and sister for thirty days. You will probably feel sorry for yourself, and you will be tempted to rail against fate, against hormones under stress, against capitalism, the Catholic Church, and God himself. If only you could understand that you are fasting.

You are fasting when you don't want to. The last thing you want is to do without. You are neither a priest nor a religious, you are both married and burning—what do you think of *that*, St. Paul?—and you are red-blooded and yearning for all life offers. Your body craves sex the way your mouth craves sweetness and your blood craves caffeine, the way, as I can personally assure you, a drying-out drunk craves one more drink. Your hormones, your crazy, stressed-out hormones, are telling you to use your lover as a fix for your carnal need, but you can't, not this month. At this moment you'd like to look the pope, God bless his dear, dear soul, in the face and say something unspeakable. You'd like to say, "Screw it all, because I can't." Your body is fasting. But there's more.

Your heart aches with insecurities and loneliness. You want to be as close to your husband as you can be, to be one flesh, to crash through the barriers of skin and bone and dissolve the ache of isolation in the closest embrace known to man. You can't. Your body and heart both must fast. You find yourself torn between obeying what you believe to your core is right and obeying your hunger.

And what of your empty arms? You long for a child. You feel like Rachel: "Give me children or I shall die!" You feel as though you would gladly hand over your heart to be broken by a horde of rough offspring, or as though you would agree to have one child for a few years and then give it back to God in death just so you could cease for a time to be a woman made barren by circumstance. You want to trash your damned monthly charts and thermometer and throw caution to the wind, go broke, become a burden on society, die in childbirth, anything but continue in this fast of body, heart, and instinct.

Wanting so much that seems a small thing to ask, you writhe in the grip of this cruel and merciless god who gives you desires only to tear from you the means of fulfilling them. Prayer withers in your mouth and your faith shrivels to a husk rattling with dead seeds; church-going becomes forced, something you do just so you won't have to go to confession again. Only your conscience holds you in place now, and, unnourished by faith, hope, and charity, you get up and shuffle in the eucharistic assembly line to the priest and swallow bread that seems drier than your soul.

You could give up half the struggle simply by rebelling, but conscience and something more than conscience hold you in place. The vise of the cruel God seems to become a pair of hands turning your head to face the crucifix. You hate it, that conventional pious image that you see dangling every day from rear-view mirrors or stuck up like a badge of membership on the walls of Catholic homes. You hate the sight of it dangling between the cool fingers of the good Catholic mothers whose virtuous ranks you long to join, but cannot join, and in your frustration you are tempted to hate them, too.

You hate the sight of the crucifix the way you hate passive suffering and the prim voice that says in your head, "Offer it up." From the edge of your eye, over in the Lady Chapel, you catch Mary's gaze. She has a patient face and a pretty red heart stuck through like a pincushion with its seven swords. *Offer it up.*

It hurts so much.

Offer it up.

I'm sorry, Mother, I just can't.

Still the hands grip your head and force you to face the crucifix till your eyes swim and that twisted gothic figure abstracts, nearly comes apart. You stare at his face, tired eyes seeking tired eyes—yes, his face appears not to be anguished, but simply *tired*. You see him, that instant, simply as an image of utter exhaustion, humiliation, failure. His poverty of spirit is complete.

What is poverty? Is it living in government housing? Is it starving Ethiopian children on television? Is it men on the street with all of their possessions heaped around them in garbage bags? Yes, and more, because there is also the poverty of absolute emptiness, of being at the end of your rope. Poor in spirit, poor as a church mouse, poor as God dying empty-handed. Well, almost: The hands are empty except for the nails.

All the anguished cries in the Bible, cries of the barren, the widows and orphans, the beggars, the blind, and the lepers begging for healing, tangle into a knot inside your brain while something in your fasting body comes loose and Mary sings, "He has looked upon his handmaid's lowliness; behold, from now on all ages shall call me blessed." And Simeon touches her hand and warns, "And a sword shall pierce your heart," predicting hundreds of years of cheap icons that show her heart like a fat satin pillow with daggers thrust in decoratively. Well, how else would an artist paint it? How do you show the pain of maternal instinct pierced through?

The Man on the cross whispers, "Blessed are the poor in spirit," and you know that this complete poverty you feel down to the roots of your being, the empty womb, empty pocket, empty heart are all you have to give him. And he will accept that.

You reach deep into the emptiness of your own disappointment and find the prayers you have not been able to pray. Offer it up? Yes, you offer your frustration and disappointment up for all of the poor, and there are so many ways of not having enough: the man on the street with all of his possessions heaped around him in garbage bags. The woman who's just had her second abortion. The woman with the deep-seated lesbianism who's trying to be chaste, or maybe not trying. The man punished for a crime he did not commit. So many people want what seems a small thing to ask, but it's still too much.

You have nothing but this poverty, and yet this poverty means so much. It is the poverty of this Man who is also completely empty, completely exhausted, with only one sigh left: It is finished. You have shared this with him, and for the moment that is enough.

I will tell you what no apologist will tell you.

Without sex, your body remembers the original aloneness in Paradise and the reason for marriage—not a hormonal itch pleasantly scratched the correct number of times a week, but completeness, the wholeness of the image of God on earth. Without a bodily expression of love, you discover the depth of a love that will outlive the body at death and survive through the resurrection of that body.

Without a child, you remember the value of life and the fact that every person on this earth, however damaged, is a gift that might not have been given. Without comfort and security, you remember that all comfort and security are illusory and that God is the only thing solid enough to lean on.

Without spiritual happiness—without even that— you discover that you can survive off a dry crust of faith. You remember the Lord of miracles with his loaves and fishes. Lord, take this dry crust and create in me a feast.

You discover, to your surprise, what it really means to be open to life.

> I said to my soul, be still, and wait without
> hope
>
> For hope would be hope for the wrong thing;
> wait without love
>
> For love would be love for the wrong thing;
> there is yet faith
>
> But the faith and the love and the hope are
> all in the waiting.

-T. S. Eliot

THERE ISN'T JUST ONE PATH TO
HEAVEN. THAT'S AS TRUE FOR GAY
CATHOLICS AS FOR OTHERS.

COMING OUT

by Eve Tushnet

When Catholics ask me why I'm so up-front about my sexual orientation, I usually answer: *somebody has to be*. Of course, it's not like I could hide it even if I wanted to. I helped found my high school's gay/straight alliance. Almost everyone who knows me knows my deal. There's no "rewind" button in real life.

I've spoken with other Catholics with homosexual desires who would never speak about it publicly. Some were members of prominent Catholic organizations, who feared losing friends and reputation. (Straight Catholics: Whose fault is that?) Others simply value their privacy and practice discretion. All are faithful to the Church's teaching, and live chastely. (One of them is perhaps the most inspiring person I've met, a man truly on fire for Christ, who brought home to me the real meaning of the Real Presence in the Eucharist.)

Virtually no one in this society will even acknowledge that it's possible to live like this. Priests don't preach this hope from the pulpit. Gay spokesmen speak as if the only alternatives are unchastity or despair—chaste queer life is one cooperation of will and grace you'll never see on *Will and Grace*. And "conservative" Christians often politely ignore fellow Christians struggling with homosexuality.

But if something exists, it must be possible; and here I am.

How I got here is another story—or two stories, actually, about coming out gay, and converting to Catholicism.

On their own, of course, neither story is exceptional. Just about every Catholic I know collects conversion stories. And just about every gay person I know collects, or collected at one point, coming-out stories. (I used to own several paperbacks dedicated solely to "How I Figured Out I Was Gay and What Happened Then" stories.) But what I've noticed is that although there are as many conversion stories and coming-out stories as there are people who tell them, these stories usually have recurring patterns and themes—in many ways, they mirror each other: They're often love stories; they're often stories in which a sense of disturbance and inadequacy provokes a search for answers, and the "answer" to the questions is found in another person—or Person. They're often stories in which an encounter with beauty forces an often unwanted recognition of a truth about oneself, one's identity, and how one needs to relate to others.

I noticed these similarities because my own conversion story seems like a bigger and much-less-wanted version of my coming-out story; and my coming-out story seems like preparation for my conversion.

Both started with the same distressing sense that something had gone wrong: I wasn't who I should be. I was raised in a very progressive household; I can't remember ever encountering any anti-gay stigma until I was in middle school. But I still, for whatever reason, connected this sense of being marred, malformed, to my sexuality and my relationships with other girls. From a very early age—this is part of my earliest memories—I felt shut out from righteousness. It was W. H. Auden's old lines, "Children afraid of the night / Who have never been happy or good."

I remember feeling like an alien, freakish, reprehensible outsider for my sexual orientation. I remember finding gay culture in books and movies and music and taking to it "like a duck to ducks," as Quentin Crisp says. I remember hiding everything I felt from myself and everyone around me. I remember that intense, sensual, paranoid awareness of how everyone around me was reacting, so I could be sure to react the same way, to react appropriately instead of reacting in a way that would expose me. (Possibly this experience has made me slightly more sympathetic to wildly desiring hetero guys, who ordinarily would really piss me off!)

I remember, too, pretty girls in their summer dresses, and the sweetness when my eyes swerved and I noticed some summer beauty. I remember seeing my semi-secret girlfriend in the hallways of our high school; I can still smell her cigarettes and her shampoo. I can still hear her voice as she explained why I had to be careful so her parents would never know we were dating. I remember developing secret languages with my best friend so we could talk about the people we had crushes on and the ways we envisioned structuring our romantic lives. I remember spending obsessive hours reading gay subtext into every single book I read and every single song I liked, so I could find someone who was like me—so I could feel that astonishing thing, like when you solve a difficult rhyming problem in an English poem, like when you pick a lock and hear all the tumblers finally shifting into place, *click-click-click*. So I could feel the door open.

Doubtless my gay identity was strongly reinforced by cultural messages that homosexuality was an intrinsic part of my soul, and that, therefore, since I desired the practice I must share the identity and make it a huge, defining part of my sense of self. I think we are far too naive about how much our culture shapes which identities we think are "real" and "deep" and "my essential true self." That's why we should focus on what we should do, and whom we should love, rather than on what we think we are.

But I don't think it's a coincidence that even before puberty, I connected my alienation with sexuality. You'll often hear conservative Christian therapists (more on them in a moment) claim that homosexuality is inevitably the result of a malformed gender identity: that gay guys failed to relate properly to other boys, and never developed a healthy masculine identity, and ditto for lesbians vs. girls. I have a lot of problems with this narrative, including its overgeneralization (what it describes is true for some people with same-sex attractions, but isn't true for everyone by a long shot), so let me make clear that I got along pretty well with other girls. Given that as a child I was primarily characterized by bad temper, selfishness, and general weirdness, I had a somewhat startling number of close female friends throughout my childhood and adolescence. I liked being a girl, and I didn't feel "different from all the other girls"; I felt different from all the other humans. Whatever was going on in my psyche—and my story is only one possible story, to which a lot of lesbians won't relate at all—it was more about sexuality, an apprehension of something troubling in one's sexual desires, than about gender identity or femininity.

Learning the words for homosexuality, gay, lesbian, came as an intense relief. Oh, if *that's* all it is . . . ! I could blame society for my alienation, and use it to fuel political activism. My best friend and I helped to start a gay/straight alliance at our high school; I went to marches, got in arguments, and generally made myself obnoxious in the way that politically minded high school students are inevitably obnoxious.

In obvious ways, the coming-out process is self-centered, caught up in attempts to make sense of oneself and one's desires. There are a lot of ways in which the entire framework of "gay identity" is based on the almost Gnostic idea of a secret, true self, opposed to the outside forces of culture or religion. But even so, developing a gay identity can focus you on longing, and so on the ways in which you're incomplete, needy.

And developing a gay identity can push you outside yourself, outside your comfort zone, to care for others, both in romantic relationships and in political comradeship. Struggle and suffering can coarsen a person's character. They can also soften and strengthen it. I've learned so much about what the latter looks like from gay men and lesbians. I need both hands to count the number of people who have told me that when they came out, their families rejected them to the point of declaring, "You're dead to me." (I've told this to "straight" people who wondered if I was making it up—surely people don't use such flamboyantly cruel language to their own children! But yeah, they do—a lot.) Eugene Debs's old catechetical formula applied to me as a gay activist, just as it applies even more strongly to me as a Christian: "While there is a lower class, I am in it. While there is a criminal element, I am of it. While there is a soul in prison, I am not free."

By the time I went to college, I thought I had a few things settled. The whole sexuality issue was basically resolved. I had figured out the meaning hidden in women's beauty: duh, you're gay (or bisexual or whatever), end of story.

In college I met, for the first time, practicing Catholics who would talk to me about why they held their bizarre beliefs. I joined a debating society with a number of these weird creatures, and found that I admired them a lot—and that they reopened some of those settled questions. In the doctrine of the Fall of

Man, they offered a different explanation for the sense of wrongness that I'd felt as long as I could remember. In the doctrine of the Creation, they offered a different explanation of the sensual beauty I found in all kinds of places, but often most intensely in women's beauty.

Both the least pleasant and the most pleasant of my experiences found explanations that weren't political or psychological, but existential: The stuff I'd been trying to figure out all my life wasn't just about me and my particular society's response to human sexual variation, but was instead about the human condition. Instead of marking me out as different from the other humans, these two experiences that had caused me to discern my sexual orientation were actually responses to the truth about all other humans, created in God's image but fallen and exiled.

I was very lucky with these people (although maybe it wasn't just luck). They didn't bother psychoanalyzing me. They didn't care why I was gay—the obsession with homosexuality's origins that grips many Christian communities had passed them by. They didn't try to explain me to myself. They didn't try to make the Christian account of alienation and beauty erase the gay account; they didn't try to say, "Oh, you're not really gay, you just think you are because x, y, or z." (That's good, because the sense of recognition I felt upon coming out was really strong. If that recognition was totally unfounded, I find it hard to understand how I could ever trust the even more shocking and demanding recognition of Christian truth.)

They did try to explain Church teachings on homosexuality because I pestered them about it. And honestly, their explanations were pretty bad. Sex should only be used for its highest purpose, in which both love and procreation can combine—well, why? We don't say it's wrong to use other gifts, like language, for reasons other than their highest purpose. The man who eventually became my sponsor into the Church compared sex to the communion chalice, which you wouldn't use to drink Corona; that's lovely, and the comparison definitely overturned some of my stereotypes of sex-hating, body-hating Catholics, but it doesn't really answer the question of why that's an appropriate metaphor for sex.

I still don't feel like I really understand it. Pope John Paul II's *Theology of the Body* makes me feel like I'm at least beginning to apprehend reasons behind the Church's prohibition on homosexual acts; one reason I find it more helpful than the apologetic explanations my friends relied on is that it doesn't actually talk about homosexuality at all. It's about marriage and what we can learn from the Genesis creation narratives. So it doesn't have that ad hoc, "we've gotta answer this somehow, but we have no idea how" feel that I get from a lot of made-to-order explanations for Church teaching on homosexuality.

In some ways even this lack of comprehension is beneficial to me, and maybe it's one way God is blessing me and working with me. (In the way that a Brillo pad works with a saucepot, I guess . . .) I had to recognize that the truth isn't the same as our arguments for the truth, and that the Church might be better than any explanation of it. I had to accept that I might not understand every-thing; this was, like most Christian experiences, very humiliating! I entered the Church with the bare mini-mum of trust: This is the church Jesus founded, the bride of Christ, and I'll listen to it even when I wouldn't have come up with the doctrine myself and don't "get it" or like it. And here, too, my early experiences had pre-pared me for Christianity: I was very used to considering that what I liked or wanted was not a good guide to truth or goodness.

Gay Christian life does require a lot of humility. But then, obviously, so does every other kind of Christian life.

And there are ways in which much of contemporary Christian discussion of homosexuality—very much including discussion from a traditional, don't-shtup-your-own-sex perspective—seems to me to focus us away from humility, and even away from Christ. To the extent that Christians rely on psychoanalytic accounts of human sexuality, we're still focusing on ourselves (or, worse, on other people whose own self-understandings we ignore).

You can find reams and reams of discussion of homo-sexuality in which it's all about malformed gender identi-ty, or bad relationships with one's parents, or any number of pop-Freudian reductions. And some people do find that those analyses reflect their experience and help them understand themselves. I find all of that stuff very foreign and unhelpful, and don't think it explains much about me at all. After all, St. Augustine didn't say that our hearts are restless until we Focus on the Family.

So maybe the most important thing about this intertwined conversion and coming-out story is that it's only one story. We're called to be saints, but the more I learn about the saints, the more I realize how wildly varied they are. There isn't just one path to heaven. That's as true for gay Catholics (or Catholics with same-sex attractions—again, I don't think there's only one possible accurate terminology) as for others. In some ways that's frightening: You do have to forge your own way, and gay Catholics don't have a whole lot of examples and guides specific to our experience. But in other ways it's comforting, since what you have to do is actually quite simple: Kneel, pray, seek God, humble yourself enough to follow the teachings he has given you through his church . . . and let the days take care of themselves.

WAS I THE ANTICHRIST? BEFORE
YOU LAUGH THIS OFF, CONSIDER
THE EVIDENCE.

EMILY ROSE'S EXORCISM —AND MINE

by John Zmirak

Had it provoked a demonic possession scare, *The Exorcism of Emily Rose* would have been following in the footsteps of Richard Donner's *The Omen*, the classic supernatural thriller which wrecked a solid year of my life. When this movie depicting the birth of a cuddly, handsome little Antichrist came out, it reportedly caused countless parents to rush home and check their children's scalps for birthmarks that spelled out "666." My guess is that those kids weren't demonic, but simply ADD; then again, I'm no theologian.

I was desperate to answer one of life's great existential questions: Was I the Antichrist? On a thirteen-year-old like me, the film had a slightly different effect. It sent me scrambling after every book I could find on the Antichrist and the "end times," most of them written by

Protestants—but that didn't stop me because I didn't know what Protestants were, had never knowingly met one, and pretty much assumed that all "religious" books were the same. They quoted the Bible, didn't they? One time I brought a parish priest a pamphlet I'd ordered from television which called the papacy the Whore of Babylon, and asked him to explain it.

"Don't read this," he explained, and took it from my hands. But I never brought good Fr. Grisaitis my copy of *The Late Great Planet Earth*, or *Satan in the Sanctuary*, or any of the other books I picked up here and there, or the lurid exposés of demonology and witchcraft I'd checked out of the public library. Instead, I buried myself in them—desperate to answer one of life's great existential questions:

Was I the Antichrist?

Before you laugh this off, consider the evidence:

- I had never quite fit in with any of the children at my blue-collar parish school—quite unlike my well-behaved and much-beloved sisters, as the teachers liked to remind me. Nor would I do any of the work assigned, unless it happened to accord with my powerful inner promptings. Punishments and threats were useless. Once a nun squatted down to face my second grade stature and scolded me at the end of the year: "You haven't done a lick of the work you were assigned this year. You deserve to be left back to repeat this grade." I stood there for a moment, running an icy calculus in my head, and replied: "But then you'd have me for an extra year. And I don't think either of us wants that." Just What Damien Would Do (WDWD).

• When I passed them in the schoolyard, laden down with encyclopedias I was reading for fun, my schoolmates would find themselves driven to chant my last name, like some infernal mantra. My appearance at a lunchroom table was enough to provoke an eerie, strained silence—just like Damien.

• I'd been born a surprise and remained an enduring shock to my almost home-bound, agoraphobic mother—who found me incomprehensible from the moment I learned to talk, and regularly swore that she had taken home "the wrong kid from the hospital." Damien's parents asked similar questions about their own little spawn of Satan.

• My poor sisters, charged with caring for me as a child, had despaired of disciplining me or influencing my behavior in any way—noting that punishments only provoked from me an escalating, incessant chant of, "I won't, I won't, I won't, and you can't make me . . . I won't, I won't, I won't . . ." They began to call me "Rosemary's baby."

• I hated the cheery, happy "folk Mass" my parents dragged me to in our grammar-school gym, with its upbeat songs and smiling nuns in pink pantsuits. When we sang "Blowin' in the Wind" by some obscure church composer named B. Dylan, I grimly read the flowery and impenetrable lyrics—and figured that they must be from the Old Testament. Then I'd sneak upstairs to the cavernous upper church to savor the darkness, the grim silence, and the smoke which reminded me of my favorite TV show, *The Addams Family*. Draw your own conclusions . . .

- I was a twelve-year-old sexual harasser. As I discovered the dawning curves of my school's young Margarets, Lisas, and Rosarias, I found I couldn't quite keep my hands off them. Not even at the girls' earnest insistence. Warnings and retaliation had no effect on me whatever. (Or on Damien.) The teachers taught me a new vocabulary word: "incorrigible."

- Worst of all, I discovered early in seventh grade that I was suffused with thoughts of . . . evil. Or, thoughts that *were* evil anyway—as I knew because I'd looked them up. As sexual fantasies swarmed through my head despite every attempt to suppress them, I began to wonder about the nature of these thoughts, and dutifully went to my favorite source—a reference book. My parents had lying around an old moral manual from 1945, translated with dogged literality from the Latin, replete with detailed information about the gravely sinful nature of "impure thoughts," "self-abuse," and other forms of "pollution," and a helpful little section on hell. I looked in vain for mitigations or exceptions, or suggestions on how to stop up this font of evil. One Saturday in confession, an elderly Spanish priest, frustrated at having heard the same sins from me the week before, threatened to deny me absolution. I stumbled out of the confessional, stunned—and not long afterward went to see *The Omen*.

And suddenly, it all made sense.

I was a twelve-year-old sexual harasser. Warnings and retaliation had no effect on me whatsoever. In *The Omen*, young Damien is born as the incarnate child of Satan himself, born evil and unable to choose otherwise. Now, this is a piece of theological nonsense; the Antichrist discussed in the Apocalypse of St. John, when he comes, will be nothing more than a particularly wicked human being. Satan is utterly powerless to emulate the Incarnation nor can he compel us to sin. (The things done by a person possessed are not attributed to his soul.) But not every Catholic thirteen-year-old knows this.

I sure didn't. As far as I could see, the fact of being overwhelmed with unquenchable desires, impossible to resist, to commit mortal sins, was a pretty compelling piece of evidence that I . . . had been born the spawn of Satan, and was doomed to spread evil throughout the world and persecute the Church until I was finally crushed by the second coming.

This put quite a damper on seventh grade. Even then, I was preparing for the sacrament of confirmation; one kid in my school, with similar obsessions, argued with the nuns that "Lucifer" should be an acceptable confirmation name because "Dude, he was an angel, right? Right?"

But I embraced my demonic destiny with no such enthusiasm. I knew enough to realize that mine was the losing side, that some day I'd end up with a Woman Clothed By the Sun crushing my head beneath her heel. And I didn't look forward to it one bit. Nor to the lake of fire, the second death, or the weeping and gnashing of teeth amidst the fire that does not die with the worm that does not sleep. I'd put on a scapular sometimes, and wonder why it didn't catch on fire.

I pondered my eternal destiny in hell all through confirmation class, which focused, naturally enough, on penmanship. Seriously. Each of us had to write a letter to Brooklyn bishop Francis Mugavero explaining why he wished to be confirmed. This being an old-fashioned Catholic school, the most important thing was neatness. Since I had terrible handwriting, I was kept after school every day for weeks, retracing the same exact words, over and over—all the while pondering St. Thomas's promise that the damned would receive back their flesh at the resurrection, "to perfect their punishment in the senses." I imagined a hot dentist drill applied to the eyes . . .

And that is when I came up with a way out—or at least a means of finding the answer. Since I had a major sacrament coming up, it could serve as an empirical test of my hypothesis. Surely the spawn of Satan himself could not sit through an entire confirmation service without blaspheming it. The incarnate spirit of evil could not receive the Holy Ghost called down upon him by the descendant of the apostles without reacting like a vampire at the sight of a crucifix. If the promptings of primal evil which filled my mind with thoughts of cleavage, stockinged calves, and secret crevices most waking hours every day were truly invincible, a sign of my destiny and nature, then nothing could stop them—not even the Holy Ghost, since Satan (as I had read) is beyond redemption. He is too fixed in evil to repent. The question, then: Was I?

So I made myself an experiment. If I could sit through the entire two-hour confirmation service without once thinking of sex, or feeling a . . . stirring . . . of the flesh, it would prove that my nature was not, in fact, demonic. If I couldn't, well that would prove the contrary. As the Jesuits used to say, *quod erat demonstratum*.

As the after-school penmanship lessons drew to a close—the nun despaired and sent my diabolical chicken scratch off to the bishop—and the great experiment approached, I had trouble getting to sleep at night. Something about the embrace of limitless darkness left me feeling too vulnerable. I awaited the day as I imagine the scientists of the Manhattan project did their first tests at Los Alamos—though of course the evil power they unleashed was nothing compared to the monstrosities I would be driven by my nature to commit, should it happen that I failed the test. I thought grimly of the mass murders, wars, and persecutions I would have to unleash, and wondered idly if I could spare Astoria, Queens, from the general wrack—particularly the rain of Wormwood with which I would be compelled to poison the seas. Could I at least save my dog?

When the big day arrived, and I donned the red polyester robes we'd been loaned, and the stole we would get to keep, I marched into the church as if to my own murder trial—for millions of murders, really, except that they lay in the future. But God, I had read, is not bound by time. In a sense, I might already be guilty of them. I sat in the pew among my classmates, and tried to ignore the girls—the flouncing hair, the bright makeup of the Italian girls, the rosy skin of the Irish. I sang the hymns in a breaking voice, and strained every nerve below the waist for a hint of arousal, of the rising gavel which would mean a guilty verdict.

And nothing happened. Chalk it up to performance anxiety, but I made it through unscathed. For the first time in over a year, I managed to keep my thoughts pure for a solid ninety minutes. The girls might have been bodiless spirits, for all I cared. They looked even—angelic. The sweaty, gum-chewing guys were not future victims of genocides for which I would be responsible, but just a pack of future cops and firemen. The bishop, I knew for a fact, would not die in prison because of me. My stony heart was once again a heart of flesh, and the Spirit was in me the same as everybody else, no more and no less. I let my parents take me for ice cream.

So I like to tell people that confirmation meant more to me than it did to anyone else I know. But I don't tell them why.

I CERTAINLY SAW AN IMAGE OF CHRIST IN THE SISTERS, BUT GETTING TO KNOW THE MEN, I STRUGGLED TO FIND AN IMAGE OF CHRIST IN THEM. THEY WERE A CANTANKEROUS BUNCH.

ENCOUNTERING THE SCOURGED CHRIST

by Jack Smith

Many years ago, for reasons I won't bother you with, I was afforded the opportunity to perform twenty hours of community service at the charity of my choice. After putting it off until the last minute, I chose the Missionaries of Charity AIDS hospice, then in San Francisco. It was close to my girlfriend's apartment.

I wasn't very eager, but the sisters welcomed me. My first responsibility was to drive the sisters to Project Open Hand and pick up food to be distributed to shut-in AIDS sufferers at 6th Street and tenderloin flophouses. Considering the neighborhoods they were serving, I was also an unofficial bodyguard. I'm six-foot-two and over 200 pounds and the sisters' height range was at the lower end of five feet. These women didn't need any bodyguard, though. They were strong and held their own in any situation.

My twenty hours ran out, but I couldn't stop coming back. I wanted to see the sisters.

The main reason the sisters did what they did was that they saw an image of Christ in all of the people they served, especially the poorest of the poor.

After my twenty hours were over, my main responsibility was to hang out with the men to talk and smoke, and drive them to the hospital for treatment.

At the entrance to the room where I hung out with the men, the sisters had a poster of Christ. It was a terribly graphic representation of him after the scourging. He wasn't the strong and serene Good Shepherd, and he wasn't the glorious risen Christ with five vague symbolic wounds. Chunks of flesh were ripped out of his body by the scourging. Blood was flowing and he was sorrowful. A caption read, "I thirst." It bothered me whenever I saw it and I thought, sarcastically, "How lovely!"

I certainly saw an image of Christ in the sisters, but getting to know the men, I struggled to find an image of Christ in them. They were a cantankerous bunch.

They complained about the sisters. They complained about their medical treatment. They convinced me to buy them cigarettes and other things with no intention of paying me back. I listened to them whine endlessly, to and from the hospital. I often had to make side trips on the way back from the hospital in order to visit a favorite restaurant or bookstore. They complained about me, and I complained about them.

Some of them had horrible stories. One had abandoned his wife and children and had acquired AIDS picking up young male prostitutes on Polk Street.

I went with the sisters once to visit a man with whom I got along particularly well. He was committed to the psych ward at S.F. General because he had tried to commit suicide twice. The sisters couldn't keep him in their residence, but they still wanted to visit him. I brought him a carton of Marlboros.

A young short Hispanic sister told me as we were waiting for the elevator to go to the dreaded fourth floor, very sincerely and in a heavy accent, "You are building a crown for yourself in heaven which can never be taken away no matter what you do."

I thought to myself, "Whatever, sister! I just drove you here and bought him some cigs."

I got to know most of the men well and enjoyed their company despite the dementia that had settled into a number of them in the last stages of their disease. There was fulfillment in my work, but not the kind the sisters had. I felt I was fulfilling my duties to Christian charity, but not that I was actually serving images of the scourged Christ.

One day I was asked to come by and take a man to the hospital to whom I'd never spoken before. Some other volunteers carried him down the steps and placed him in the passenger seat of my Chevy Blazer.

I drove him alone to S.F. General and he spent most of the time thanking me and telling me how important prayer had become in his life. By the look of him, that life was about to end and I had no expectation of taking him home from the hospital. I don't know what his story was or how he arrived in the position he was in. He had a growth the size of a baseball in his groin, he couldn't walk, he was gaunt and in pain.

I paid little attention and was fearing our arrival at the hospital because I knew I would have to lift him out of my high SUV seat to put him in his wheelchair.

On arrival, I went to lift him and was surprised at how easy it was; he was all bones. I was also surprised when I felt something wet and then looked at my car-seat as I was pulling him out. He had urinated on my seat!

He groaned a bit in pain as I lifted him down from the car and kept saying "I'm so sorry, I'm so sorry. Thank you, thank you."

I was upset and extremely uncomfortable and then something hit me like a ton of bricks. I plopped him in his wheelchair and spun him around quickly so he wouldn't see my tears.

This greatly suffering man, soon to die, had long hair, a beard and purple splotches covering his body. I had just held the scourged Christ.

And He was lovely.

"LET ME TELL YOU SOMETHING," HE
SAID TO ME. "I ADMIRE YOUR IDEAL-
ISM. BUT IN ABOUT FIVE YEARS,
MAYBE SOONER, YOU ARE GOING
TO BURN OUT AND QUIT."

THE HARSH AND DREADFUL LOVE OF THE POOR

by Marion Maendel

It's another suffocating Houston night. Air, warm and thick as smoke, cloaks the city and settles in folds between the buildings on Rose Street. I sit in my second-story room in Casa Juan Diego House of Hospitality, fan stirring the heat, and read my journal of two years ago.

The entries cover my first months' experience here, and the writing is definitely familiar. The leaky green pen I remember as well, but the words printed across the college-ruled notebook are those of a stranger. Who is this naïve do-gooder, so clinically diagnosing "problems in society" and outlining plans for "helping others"? And those dreams, the square solid expectations and fluffy quotes about serving the poor—I can't even imagine what they once meant. Smiling, I turn the page.

Outside in the night, a police siren shatters the heavy stillness. My ceiling twirls with red and blue flashing lights, and without looking, I can visualize the scene below my window. Two or three men, quite drunk, lie with cheeks pressed to the warm concrete, hands cuffed behind them, as an officer barks commands in very bad Spanish. Leaning into the shadow of the laundromat wall, a handful of the male prostitutes are snickering quietly.

I return to the journal. It's littered with words as empty as the pages they're written on: "world suffering," "the poor," "social transformation." My eyes wander over a tidy commentary on "justice," then drift again with the heavy thump and twang of Tejano music coming from next door. That's Sonia's room. She's a sweet, dark-eyed sixteen-year-old from El Salvador, battered and pregnant by her twenty-three-year-old "boyfriend." And homeless. And scared.

Again I try to concentrate. But now a gasp like a knife comes through the thin drywall, and sobbing—hard, choked, muffled in a pillow—follows after. It mocks the crisp words in front of me. I stand up and shut off the fan.

"Sonia, *m'ija*, what's up?"

The journal lands in the trash.

I have begun my third year here as a Catholic Worker. Arriving at Casa Juan Diego fresh out of high school, I had the classic "messiah complex," and felt ready to save the world. Becoming a member of a vibrant volunteer movement equipped with enormous facilities, and widely known in the Hispanic community, did little to convince me otherwise. As I immersed myself in Catholic Worker philosophy, study, and discussions, I became enamored with the idea of "serving the poor" and "working for justice."

Then I met the people. They were poor, yes, and undeniably oppressed, downtrodden and desperate. I had counted on that. But I was unprepared for their concrete humanity, their sheer individuality as persons. They refused to be categorized as passive "problems" simply because I had appointed myself "helper." My well-heeled, condescending donation of time and surplus kindness was despicable in their eyes, and they were not desperate enough to bow and scrape around it for survival's sake.

It was the very people I came to "help" who began to teach me that acknowledgement of our common humanity under the pure gaze of God was the first and only point at which our mutual liberation could blossom. "We must be saved together," I read from Dorothy Day, and the smooth shell of my idealism began to splinter.

A year went by. On the plane trip back from summer vacation, I found myself sitting next to a businessman, who introduced himself as the CEO of a massive German graphic arts company.

"I'm a Catholic Worker volunteer," I nodded and quickly outlined the CW movement.

Reinart was fascinated. "Tell me about your work, the people," he begged. I told. He was silent and gazed out the window for a moment. "Let me tell you something," he said finally. "I admire your courage. I admire your idealism. But I will predict something, too. In about five years, maybe sooner, you are going to burn out and quit."

A little question mark of worry began to tingle in my stomach. It had been a long, luxurious vacation in the country. The thought of returning to inner-city sordidness was suddenly terribly tiring, the endless dark parade of problems and demands, terrifying.

"Maybe," I conceded. "But how so?"

"Easy. You are going to run out of idealism first. You are going to become hard and cynical, and realize that people are cruel and thankless and undeserving SOBs. And then you'll get a real job."

I stared at the seat in front of me. I thought of Marina, a battered woman with two children we had taken in a year ago. Besides giving her unlimited time with us to reorganize her life, we'd arranged work for her, counseling sessions, medical care, and legal assistance. One day she went to a close priest friend of ours, crying that we'd kicked her out without warning, and never done a thing to help. I remembered Vinny, who had run away from our youth house one night, taking with him every single one of our hard-won, portable electrical appliances. The seat in front of me blurred.

"Reinart," I said, "I think my idealism ran out my first month at work."

He nearly choked on his coffee. Reinart could respectfully dismiss my transient idealism, but the possibility of another sustaining force had his immediate attention.

"So what's left?" he demanded, and his eyes were suddenly fierce.

"Absolutely nothing." The words came hard, but I knew in that moment of resignation a relief as fine and pure as cold water. In acknowledging that my shaky fortress of idealism now lay in ruins, I finally allowed myself to be vulnerable. My "I know, you don't" approach to those whom I intended to save crumpled, and I became weaker, not more elite.

I was shocked to discover that I, too, was desperately needy, empty, poor. And with the death of my belief in "the cause," came the assurance of another sort of stability, this no longer blind and shifting, but open, painfully open, and solid like a rock. Into that gaping wound rushed a healing liberation, a new forgiveness, a fresh capacity to love and be loved in faith, with God as the Source of compassion this time, not myself. It is a faith I still do not wholly possess, but it flits above the outstretched hand of my heart like a bright butterfly, and I know it to be the truth.

To have the vision in our hearts and minds of a new social order where love and justice truly reign is imperative, yes. This vision is usually what compels us to examine our lives so that we may live, work, and love in a manner consistent with the kingdom of God, and it can reveal to us the concrete, practical ways of conversion.

But if such a vision remains in the abstract realm alone, it is useless, and eventually becomes an obstacle to any real transformation or liberation, whether personal or social.

It is easy to be in love with a concept—"mankind," "the poor," "the masses"—for such abstractions hold all the seductiveness and untainted security of a fantasy. But when they encounter the concrete man, the concrete poor person, their cleanness is revealed as emptiness, their whiteness as sterility, and their sweetness as a cheap perfume that evaporates too quickly.

Tolstoy tells the story of a trainload of Communist agitators on their way to a Siberian labor camp. All of them have glorious dreams for the creation of a new society, where each will live in beatific harmony, justice, and peace with his neighbor. But so removed are their ideals from the filth and chaos and humanity around them that they cannot translate them into a single loving action. As the train rattles on through the icy night, they refuse to even make eye contact.

The inevitable disillusionment we experience early on in our journey here leaves us in a bleak, inner winter, but we can allow its empty ground to provide the spring seedbed for a truer love, the "harsh and dreadful love" talked of by Dostoyevsky and Dorothy Day. This love is active, with little use for visionary dreaming.

If I truly believe in the dignity of the human being, then I must also believe in the dignity of the bag lady waiting in our entrance hall, who complains that she doesn't like what I got her for dinner, and demands a tour of the accommodations before settling in. If I want to write about justice on my computer, I need to realize that the extra sweatshirts in my closet are property belonging to Sonia next door.

Purely philosophical dreams of love and justice are only given meaning when we begin to know poor people as people, and not obstacles, or objects to be acted upon. Then, slowly perhaps, can a society where love and justice flourish as by-products begin to grow. Cuban-American theologian Roberto Goizueta has called this phenomenon the "scandal of particularity," where only the option for poor persons, not "the poor" exists.

The particular is indeed a scandal. "People come to join us in our 'wonderful work,'" Dorothy Day once said. "It all sounds very wonderful, but life itself is a haphazard, untidy, messy affair." Here we are confronted with inconveniences, frustrations, and concrete rewards unknown to dreams. Helping a child walk for the first time, celebrating survival on New Year's Eve with a group of battered women, appreciating the relief of a starving, footsore immigrant family as they collapse on the sofas in the entrance after weeks of walking attest to a gospel message rooted in the sacramentality of the human experience.

Faced with such raw distress, we must sometimes let go of all preconceived responses to a person's difficulties, including the desires to play savior or superman, and only let the pain rip into our hearts like a pruning hook. We must let it slash off the dead limbs of our coldness, cynicism, and self-dependency to prepare for the new growth of compassion. Sometimes all we can do is weep in the brokenness of our human condition.

In this spirit, we learn with our guests to accompany the condemned Jesus of the poor, who wept for the world.

Rather than let our lack of answers drive us to despair or anger, we can simply weep with and for Ricardo, whose teenage son was killed in gang crossfire; for Sara, fifteen, raped, pregnant, and kicked out of her house by incredulous parents; for Lupe, with her eyes swollen shut from spousal abuse; for Agustino, who rang the clinic doorbell yesterday, blood dripping from his clumsily slashed wrists—"I did it, I did it again"—his eyes huge with a child's terror.

Some nights I hold my head and ask myself, and God, what it is I think I'm doing here. We are, in the countless eyes of our critics, a foolishly blind group of idealists, obsessed with band-aid work. No amount of food, clothing, shelter, the "works of mercy," can stop the flow of desperate people that pours through our door. No amount of love, understanding, patience, giving, can immunize against the cruelty of human nature.

And yet, when I feel we can give no longer, when I want to turn my back on the whole business, when my utter inability to love frightens me so, and the futility of perseverance jeers, then, in that singular moment of brokenness, comes the still, small voice of the spat-upon Christ. And it chides me for thinking I can do this on my own, for hoping I can change people when I cannot even change myself.

It shows up my small, cold heart, which I don't want to see, and then it offers me the redemptive love of God forever young, which gives of itself, and gives, and gives, and gives and gives, without weighing the benefit, without considering the worthiness of the recipient, without imposing conditions and worldly calculations of immediate results. And in that "useless" poverty of inefficient love, and only in it, I can go on.

Thus we work out our liberation with fear and trembling. And laughter. And hope. And we each cast our little pebble, as Dorothy said, into the pool of humanity, and watch the rings expand, knowing that in God's upside-down kingdom, every menial task done in this love is graced with an eternal significance.

Several days ago I was working in the dental clinic assisting with a routine filling on Julio, a street crack addict who worked nights as a prostitute. As I took his patient bib off, and told him we were done, he continued to sit in the chair.

"What is it?" I asked.

He shook off the daze and got up. Then he picked up his baseball cap, put it on firmly backward, walked to the door and turned back.

"I guess . . . *pues*, I've just never been treated this well before."

His grin was crooked, and he was near tears.

BUT WHY DO IT? THE LONG WAIT, THE UNDRESSING, THE WAITING DAMPLY IN SEMI-NAKEDNESS, THE PLUNGE INTO FREEZING WATER WHILE MUTTERING AN *AVE MARIA*— ALL THIS, REGULARS CHEERFULLY ADMIT, IS EXTREMELY UNPLEASANT. THE IDEA, IT SEEMS, IS PENANCE.

NAKED: INTO THE WATERS OF VULNERABILITY AT LOURDES

by Austen Ivereigh

To bathe or not to bathe? That was the question. Here I was, for the second time in Lourdes, and the first time as a pilgrim with my diocese. Last time, I had been too busy reporting on Pope John Paul's spectacular finale to his traveling papacy; now, the queues, at least for the men, were not onerous. The most *lourdais* of rituals beckoned.

But why do it? The long wait, the undressing, the waiting damply in semi-nakedness, the plunge into freezing water while muttering an *Ave Maria*—all this, regulars cheerfully admit, is extremely unpleasant. The idea, it seems, is penance.

But not all sacrifices are salvific, a matter which God cleared up when he asked to be excused from tedious liturgies and sacrifices involving the incineration of cattle (see Amos 5). And I had already done, the day before, a

Stations of the Cross on the hill above the Grotto, atoning (yes, in the heat and dust) for my own transgressions and not a few of the globe's.

And just whose idea was it, this ritual? Our Lady asked Bernadette to "go drink at the spring and bathe in its waters", but "wash yourself" is just as good a translation, and rather more easily carried out under one of the Grotto taps with a few wet slaps on the cheeks. And what of Our Lady also instructing Bernadette to kiss the ground and eat the grass? Only popes do the first, and no one ever suggests that pilgrims to Lourdes should chew the fields.

But then I pondered the story. The earth, when Bernadette obeyed on February 25, 1858, was muddy; the grass was bitter; the water brackish. Onlookers who accompanied her up to this, the ninth apparition, were appalled to see her scratching the ground and acting like an animal. If these were the scandalous instructions of the Mother of God, for which Bernadette was slapped and led before the public prosecutor, who was I to object? The message transformed the young asthmatic seer, who thenceforth began to pray for the conversion of sinners.

Self-abasement, after all, is God's chosen method of saving humanity. We Catholics believe in human dignity, but only because we can embrace, like our Master, human indignity.

I was wobbling, you see. And then, over a *biere formidable*, I had found myself convinced by Fr. Chris Vipers, the diocese's charismatic Lourdes pilgrimage director.

"It's about becoming a child again," he told me. "Trusting others. You're naked and dependent, at that moment, on others to hold you and immerse you. It's about admitting your vulnerability. It's about trust. And surrender."

The prototype gospel of Lourdes is Luke's account of the paralytic being lowered through a roof by his friends into the healing presence of Jesus. That is how the sick come to Lourdes—with enormous difficulty, carried by others, trustingly. But it doesn't take long to realize that what the *malades* accept, as it were, *faute de mieux*, is what the rest of us pilgrims are invited to embrace too, spiritually speaking. Healing happens when, like Bernadette, we put aside our ego-armored selves and trust in our Creator. Hence the baths: they have emerged, over time, as the essential physical ritual of Lourdes, one that opens the heart and mind to grace. The bath is not a sacrament, but it is sacramental, an act of immersion in much the same way as the Eucharist is an act of incorporation.

Thus theoried up, I found myself queuing in the hot sun, elbowed by Italians even shorter than me, and then shuffling along a bench that snaked round toward the entrance of the baths. Every time eight men disappeared inside, we moved closer, in the manner of an old-fashioned confessional queue. The *malades*, along with the clergy, are fast-tracked in: they enter on crutches and in chariots, in the company of cheerful *hospitaliers*.

Gloria patri et filio . . .

Here we all were, some sixty men from the Euro-Catholic belt, mostly middle-aged, but a smattering of

141

young, grunting the rosary, staring at our feet as if awaiting a test for testicular cancer. In 2004, more than twice as many women (266,583) as men (121,715) took up the Virgin's invitation. Hence the disparity in facilities: there are seventeen baths in total: eleven for women and six for men.

A paralyzed man, it occurs to me, cannot move, but he is far from passive. He can refuse to be moved, or he can ask to be. We are all paralyzed and crippled by our self-righteous autonomy. We all need to trust, to let ourselves be moved, to allow ourselves to become dependent.

"*Prima volta*?" I ask my Italian neighbor. He came once before, fifteen years ago, he tells me. Right now, twice in fifteen years seems excessive.

A boy on a stretcher-chair has his hands in the air, twisted grotesquely in the classic sign of the severely disabled.

Laudate, laudate, laudate Maria, a man is urging us to sing.

"What language is that?" an Englishman behind me asks.

"That's Latin," his friend ventures.

"Oh, really?"

The stretcher carts are lined up now, contraptions from a bygone age. One is occupied by a very frail old man, his hands purple and gnarled. As the rosary switches to German, one of our number backs out, leaving quickly, shame-faced. Perhaps he has lost touch with his inner child. I am tempted, for a moment, to follow him. This trust stuff is demanding.

Hell Merry, fool of grease, zee lawd is weez you, comes a voice over the loudspeaker.

"Is that Latin too?" the voice behind me asks.

"No, I think that's English."

"Oh, really?"

Out comes a Down syndrome boy, face creased with smiles. He gives us all a thumbs-up. *Nothing to worry about, fellas,* he seems to say.

The Catholic Church is nowhere better represented than here, at this moment. The boundaries between physical and spiritual are collapsed, and the kingdom breaks out: the disabled mingle with the able-bodied, the nations mix, and we tap into God's goodness by physical acts which we are confident are not meaningless. Our literal age has little time for this stuff, which shrivels under the cold glare of rationalism. But the sacramental imagination is bigger, deeper, and wider.

All I have done is move down a pew or two, but I am much closer to what this is all about. Our unconscious grasps what our eyes cannot. Who are they, in the chariots in front of us now? Our fears—deformation, paralysis, fragility—but also our glory: the Spirit of God, assuring us of human empathy and supernatural transcendence. Healing is collective; we are in need of others. The fellow in the middle with the purple fingers could go at any time, but what better way than like this, carried by gentle young helpers, into the arms of God?

A young Westminster priest sits on the fast-track clergy bench. His open breviary reminds me to stop taking notes and be present to the moment. *There is a sliver of ice in the heart of every writer*, Graham Greene once said—and he should know. So I melt mine by pondering my intentions: a friend's imminent baby; frail and elderly relatives; a despairing friend.

"Any tips, Sean?" I ask a friendly "red cap," as the wheelchair-pushing volunteers are known.

"It's humiliating and unpleasant," says Sean, grinning. "But think of the fact that since the 1850s millions of people before you have done the same. And you're somehow connected with all of them."

Inside, my parish priest leaves one cubicle and a finger protrudes from the next one, motioning for me. Four young men in blue overalls—*brancardiers* in the Lourdes argot—and four men sitting in their underpants on chairs. I get the idea, and divest. An elderly man in a wheelchair is brought in. "So what we're going to do," the English *brancardier* gently tells him, "is to remove your shoes and socks. Then your trousers. Then your shirt." He taps each of the articles. "But we're going to leave your underpants on—for the moment."

In the chair next to me, an old man is asked if he wants just to be splashed, or dropped all the way in.

"I've been coming here since 1950," he answers, blimpishly. "I want to go right in. All the way."

Right in? All the way? How deep is this thing?

The wheelchair-bound man was gently disrobed, until all that was left were his underpants and a catheter tied to a bag of urine strapped to his pallid, blue-veined left leg. I shuddered for a moment at the description of the bath water in *Lourdes*, Emile Zola's bestselling anticlerical tract.

> As some hundred patients passed through the same water, you can imagine what a horrible slop it was at the end. There was everything in it: threads of blood, sloughed-off skin, scabs, bits of cloth and bandage, an abominable soup of ills. . . . The miracle was that anyone emerged alive from this human slime.

My turn. A deep stone bath, tiled in the Virgin's blue, with (phew!) clean water, all overseen by the Immaculate Conception. Three more *brancardiers*. Turn to the wall, I was told, and remove your underpants. As I did so, a freezing wet towel was put round my waist. The shock of the cold made me turn round too soon, and a *brancardier* to shield his eyes in mock horror.

I stepped in, and was told to make a prayer to Our Lady. A humble child I was; defenseless, powerless, borderless. A moment of great psychic and physical vulnerability, but I trust these strangers.

I rattle off a Hail Mary, forgetting my intentions.

Arms grip me. Down I go. Splash—the shock of the cold. Then up. Pants back on. Out. Change. No towel, because by tradition the water is deemed unwet.

Back into the sun, and the pious chaos of the Grotto. I find a patch of sun-kissed grass. The water has dried, soaking me in peace.

Our Lady of Lourdes, pray for us.

UNLESS WE LEARN THE JOY AND
THE HOPE OF OUR FAITH AND
EXPRESS IT THROUGH LAUGHTER,
THEN, I BELIEVE, WE ARE GOOD FOR
NOTHING AND NO DIFFERENT FROM
ANYBODY ELSE.

LAUGHTER WILL SAVE THE WORLD

by John Jalsevac

ANGELS FLY BECAUSE THEY TAKE THEMSELVES LIGHTLY.

—G. K. Chesterton

"Sometimes I see things, or hear things, that are just so beautiful, so infinitely beyond my understanding, that I don't know how else to respond to them except with laughter. I hardly know why this is, but for me it's the most natural expression of awe and appreciation."

Here I am, sitting with an ice-cold Guinness in my right hand, rocking back and forth on a porch swing on a third-story balcony, trying again to articulate my newly developed, and developing, theory of laughter. I have the acute sense that it isn't going well; it never really does.

"I used to think that this was normal," I continue, "but I've found that very few people understand what I mean; especially when I explain that sometimes the pleasure of breathing alone can be enough to make me rock with laughter."

Ypsilanti, Michigan, is a distant suburb of Detroit, and the sort of ancient neighborhood that's cast in the shadows of venerable oaks, ten feet thick. The pot-holed streets are lined with the sort of decrepit, semi-colonial houses that old witches are supposed to live in. It is also the quintessential university party town. The street, three floors below me, is lined with dozens of fraternity and sorority houses.

Between my feet rests a green flowerpot. Three half-grown specimens of the *cannabis sativa* plant sprout from its soil. They've been there for the last two hours and I long ago stopped taking any notice of them; they may as well have been petunias. The initial thought is that they add a nice splash of organic hue to the stark, peeling white paint of the balcony, which they do.

"You can only smoke the female plants," it had been explained to me a little while before.

The one doing the explaining was my friend Jonathon, who sits to my right: twenty-two years old, with the face of someone immeasurably older and eyes violently blue and electric—and sad. "I don't know how many of them are female plants. I'll have to wait to see if they flower," he continued to explain, proudly calling attention to the conspicuous greenery.

In response to my question he enumerated any of the various ways that a grown marijuana plant can be squeezed of its THC: steeped in teas, baked into any sort of baked good, chewed, smoked, etc.

Now he reclines in his chair. He doesn't yet understand my theory of laughter. I'm not surprised because I've rarely heard him laugh, and certainly not in the way I'm thinking of; that, and I'm explaining it poorly, and hardly understand it myself. But I'm warming to my topic.

A friend of over two years, at times Jonathon and I have been quite close. I'm unsurprised at his choice in illegal horticulture: disappointed, but not surprised. During the year when I lived in Ypsilanti I used to accompany him to AA meetings; not from any need of my own, but to offer him the assistance of a supportive friend, and out of curiosity and a desire to explore and to learn.

Jonathon is one of the smartest people I know. For six hours I swing back and forth, with the chain creaking at the spot where the swing is screwed into the overhang. In front of us the sun sinks below the horizon, while with a series of deft parries and thrusts and other such fencing techniques we discuss, debate, and argue about everything from drugs, to religion, to politics—and now, laughter and happiness.

There's much that we agree on. But still, I can't shake the sensations of darkness and sadness and confusion that always overcome me when confronted with someone else's sadness.

Besides accompanying Jonathon to AA meetings, the two of us habitually went to Mass together. Then— himself nineteen and myself seventeen—he was what AA members apparently arbitrarily call "recovered." After years of seeking solace in acid, ecstasy, marijuana, and alcohol, having his first taste of a drug-induced euphoria at the age of eleven, Jonathon had been "clean" for over two years.

He no longer goes to Mass. He's no longer "clean." He now ascribes to the vague, ethereal, despairing "spiritual-ity" of drug users. Though we never broach the topic, I've heard from a mutual friend that he is using acid again, one of the most destructive and dangerous of illegal drugs.

Over our six-hour conversation he weaves for me the illusion that he's still clean, that he only occasionally smokes marijuana. I don't bother to pry deeper because I see no advantage in it. I know that mere words won't ever convince him to drop his addiction; something deeper, something of grace is the only thing that can accomplish that miraculous feat.

On one level I understand and empathize with Jonathon; I think that's why I've been friends with so many recovering and recovered, and sometimes active, addicts. And yet, there's also that other something in me that wants so desperately to grab him and shake him and say: "Don't you see how sad you are? Don't you see that you're ruining yourself? Don't you see? Don't you want to be happy? Let me tell you about happiness. Let me tell you about happiness, about joy."

But how? I don't have the words—me, a man of words—and I know it, and I feel terrifyingly impotent. So I try to explain my newfound, embryonic theory of laughter, which is a theory of joy. Still, I know that words will never adequately make him, or anyone, understand.

With a sweep of his hand, when we're discussing drugs and certain ideas surrounding them, Jonathon indicates the rooftops of the dozens of frat houses. "There isn't a house here that isn't growing the stuff," he says, meaning marijuana. I know that he's right; I've been to the parties at these places, after all.

Jonathon, in fact, is archetypal of my generation. Mine is a generation of addicts; if there is an addiction, we have it, in droves: addiction to drugs—both legal and illegal—to alcohol, to computer games, to television, to sex, to masturbation, to pornography.

But why? Why is this the case?

Let me try to explain.

Last week, just before the summer came to an end and I left my full-time job as a journalist, I sat at my computer, reading endless reams of news articles. As I did, I stumbled upon an essay. It is a famous essay, a devastating essay, and I believe it's still often read for having captured in a single pass the collective apocalyptic mindset of the Cold War generations.

On the news that night, Lewis Thomas, the Cold War essayist, the facts-at-his-fingertips newsman, said that with proper preparation maybe the Soviet Union could only kill forty, instead of eighty, million Americans with their nuclear bombs; if only Americans were prepared to flee out of the cities to the countryside in time. And then America could retaliate and obliterate the USSR.

"If I were sixteen or seventeen," concluded Thomas, "and I had to listen to that, or read things like that, I would want to give up listening and reading . . . I would be twisting and turning to rid myself of human language."

But upon further reflection I've concluded that Thomas didn't go far enough. I think what he should have said is that he would be twisting and turning to rid himself not only of language but of thought altogether. He really should have said that he would be twisting and turning to squeeze out of the tight, claustrophobic scales of his self-awareness, if he was sixteen or seventeen and had to read and listen to things like that.

I was reading the news earlier tonight. "Al-Qaeda nukes already in United States," said one of the headlines. "Bin Laden's goal is to kill at least four million Americans, two million of whom must be children."

"China is prepared to use nuclear weapons against the U.S. if it is attacked by Washington during a confrontation over Taiwan," said another.

And another still: "At least fifty people have been killed in suicide bombings in London."

These, I think, are only a few examples of the most obvious reason why my generation is a generation of addicts. They are why we are a generation that laughs so seldom, or why when we do laugh it's not the hearty laugh of joy, but the shrill laugh of despair.

We're addicts because we're surrounded by evils so insidious and so subtle, as perhaps the world has never seen before.

But unlike Lewis Thomas, who was writing from the distant platform of middle age, tenuously casting his mind into the perspective of adolescence, I can explicitly recall what it was like to be sixteen or seventeen; it was only three years ago.

At seventeen I was not happy. I was not happy for many and diverse reasons. Mostly I suppose it was because I barely believed in God, and sometimes not at all, and for a time, because of Descartes and others with strangely alluring ideas, I believed not even in the physical world.

But now, three years later, I've concluded that to deny God and even the physical world is untenable on every level. I have concluded that I must replace the selfish self-destructiveness of my adolescence with something altogether different.

Chesterton made me do it. Somehow despite a reading list several miles long, I never discovered this giant of Catholic literature until I was eighteen. I don't remember who introduced me to him, but after reading as much of the jolly Brit as even the strongest disposition can handle, I've concluded that his is the ethos of laughter. This is also, I think, necessarily the ethos of humility. In many ways Chesterton himself is the embodiment of the words of St. Francis, whom Chesterton quotes in *The Meaning of the Crusade*: "Shall I, the gnat that dances in Thy ray, dare to be reverent?"

I, too, want so much to laugh like Chesterton laughed, like St. Francis is purported to have laughed.

And yet now, as this long, long, hot summer progresses toward its end, something has again changed. A new shadow has fallen across my soul. It has become a part of my job as a journalist to be well informed. Every day, after my editor has assigned my two or three stories for the day, I have to read dozens and dozens of news articles. This was never the case before; I have never been "well informed" before.

And as my mind and my store of experiences grow, I find my tenuous personal peace being repeatedly shattered by the force of crashing revelations that I wouldn't ever have expected. This summer—with information and events from throughout the world pouring in a turgid river into my mind—has been rammed with such intrusive revelations.

I've seen a man shoot himself up with drugs, but never before an entire nation. I've known a man to commit suicide, but never before an entire continent. I've known individual men whose souls have been a pool of darkness, but never have I so completely faced the black spots on the soul of man.

This summer, in my capacity as a journalist, I have had to see and write about all of these things.

The fact is, though I desperately want to live the ethos of laughter, I am now gripped by the ethos of fear. I find this a curious and terrible thing because I thought that Chesterton and the saints had finally taught me the greatest and most enduring lesson of my life. I thought that maybe nothing in the world could make me stop laughing, not even death, and certainly not something so ridiculous as evil. But if I have stopped laughing, I who have known in a sometimes sublime manner the deep comfort of faith, how much more so the rest of my poor, disillusioned generation?

Sometimes, in fact, when I now read the news I find myself twisting and turning to shake off thought. The other night was one of those nights. That night as I studied the horror of the day's events, I imagined bombs strapped to the bodies of strong, young Arab men, and I imagined Chinese and American and British missiles peacefully slicing through the air hundreds of miles above the earth; I imagined terrifying explosions in New York, in London, in Beijing, in Baghdad, in Baghdad, in Baghdad. In Washington, in Moscow, in Los Angeles.

More terrifying still, I imagined babies born into test-tubes and wantonly destroyed by the tens of thousands, or being torn apart in the womb, and I imagined the dignified sick and elderly and disabled left to die, slowly and alone. My nightmares now are filled with the grinning visages of such demonic things.

I recall a conversation I had earlier this year with a friend of mine, Christina, who, like me, is a student of philosophy. It was a conversation conducted under the dome of nature's great cathedral and it continued late into the night.

At one point she leaned back and looked up at the whirling stars and to my surprise murmured that sometimes she, who I had thought was supremely at peace in every way, was tempted to believe it true that indeed "ignorance is bliss." It is, I've since come to know, a common temptation among my fellow philosophy students; or rather, it is a common temptation among those who dare to think, and especially now, in this day and age.

Sometimes I, too, and even now, as I sit here on this porch with Jonathon, with his marijuana plants growing up between my feet, I am hit with the temptation to pursue the bliss of ignorance. I think that maybe I should be smoking up; shooting juice into my thirsty veins; indiscriminately folding myself into the ecstatic pleasure of others' bodies; losing myself in the non-intelligence of sensual ecstasy through whatever means available—I should join my generation in their restless orgy of forgetfulness. I think that I should be squeezing out of thought altogether, not just reading and listening; that I want to squeeze out of thinking, to shed that rotten skin.

A number of weeks ago I attended a party hosted by a good high-school friend of mine; in the midst of the natural intoxication of that sweet summer night a dozen boys and girls only a little younger than myself sat around a table and passed around a large, potent marijuana joint. And they drank. They drank with a curious desperation, as though every sip was vital to their continued existence at that precise moment.

At one point in the night I distinctly recall coming face to face with one of these boys, about seventeen or eighteen, whose ghostly pale, uncomprehending face leered with an expression of such anarchy that I was unconsciously compelled to step away from him.

Sitting on the subway a few days ago on my way to the office, I heard a group of students about my age discussing the various anti-depressants and drugs that have been prescribed to them. I wasn't surprised—far too many of my friends are on the stuff—but it saddened me nonetheless. A close friend of mine, whom I'll call Sarah, has attempted suicide on at least three occasions—whether to seek attention or to seek the embrace of death I don't know; but after each attempt she is stuffed with new drug cocktails. She blithely accepts the prescriptions.

This is my generation. My generation twists, and it turns and it squirms; they're not listening, and they're certainly not reading and most of the time, if they can help it, they're not even thinking.

"I've been thinking about it a lot," I say to Jonathon as the dying sun pierces through the leaves of the giant oak across the street. By now I am working on my second pint of Guinness, and happy because I'm beginning to understand my topic better than I ever have before.

"People laugh all the time, but are usually unable to put into words the reason why they do. But I've looked into it, and I think that everybody agrees that humans laugh mostly on account of incongruities. For instance, as Chesterton says somewhere in one of his essays, men will laugh when a prime minister sits on his hat, not because the prime minister has spoiled his hat, but because the dignity of the man and especially his office makes it so absurd that he should do something so base as to sit on his hat."

It's difficult to explain exactly what I mean, and I'm struggling to put it into words. Hilaire Belloc, I think, sums up what I'm trying to say so beautifully when he says in *The Path to Rome*, in a quote that my moral theology professor repeats at least once every class: "We laughers have a gross cousinship with the most high, and it is this contrast and perpetual quarrel which feeds a spring of merriment in the soul of a sane man."

This is a rich quote, and forces an immense amount of truth into a very few words. But it explains so well why I have sometimes laughed so ecstatically, sometimes just at the beauty of the act of breathing, and often at the beauty of a landscape, or the face of the girl I love.

I laugh because of God's greatest joke on the whole universe; I laugh because of this strange contrast, the incongruity between my humanity and my divinity, and the incongruity of a limited physical world that still manages in some mysterious way to contain and emanate Infinity himself. This divine joke is necessarily hidden in every bit of the universe, from the breath we take into our lungs, to the majestic peak of Mount Everest, and everything else in between.

But here's the kicker. Here, I think, is the whole root of the problem. If—as we're all taught to believe in this modern age—if I'm the sole shaper of my destiny, if I'm not answerable to anything outside of my own self, if I'm the paragon of all of reality, if, in short, I am god, then that humorous and beautiful incongruity of the similarity and dissimilarity between me and the Most High can only be perceived as a grotesque lie arbitrarily woven into the fabric of the universe. Then I must follow one of two paths: either to ignore this divine joke, to pretend as if it didn't exist, or to try to overcome it, to prove that I am god. Either option can only lead to despair, because in both cases I am picking a fight with reality, and reality (which is truth) will always win.

The fact is that man is a humorous creature, an awkward amalgam of corruptible matter that will pass away, and an eternal soul that is capable of sharing in the inner life of the triune God. Man straddles time and eternity in such a way that if ever he were to step back and observe his own position, he would roar with a hearty and appreciative laughter. We are God's greatest and most sublime joke because we're *not* God, and yet we do have a "gross cousinship with the most high," and "it is this contrast and perpetual quarrel which feeds a spring of merriment in the soul of a sane man."

We're no longer able to laugh at this joke infused into the universe by God himself. Because of man's failed attempt to set himself up as his own god, we're no longer able to take ourselves lightly, to put ourselves in the proper context within the cosmos, so that we might fly like the angels mentioned by Chesterton, that we might laugh at and with ourselves as the saints do, and discover that we are soaring upward towards our Maker.

The night of that party I listened to the hollow, hyenic laughter of the drug-stuffed scarecrows that sat around that table and its sadness made me want to weep. "They have made laughter lonelier than tears," says Chesterton.

What can you say to convince them that maybe thinking can show them a far deeper and more fundamental joy than their false and empty ecstasy? This question torments me because they seem to be spiraling in an impervious orbit, heedlessly circling beyond my reach.

It occurred to me that night that maybe, even as my friends were lost within their languishing, drug-induced trance, if they heard the deep, welling, humble, consciousness-smashing laughter of a saint, perhaps that would cut through the layers upon layers of walls they've constructed around their minds. Perhaps, just perhaps, that kind of a true thing crashing into their world of illusions would collapse their house of cards. Perhaps it would startle them and make them stop and listen for just a moment. My generation no longer wants to listen or read or think. It is squirming and twisting and turning to stop itself from thinking. It wants nothing to do with thought; it looks on thought as an enemy. The true laugh may be the only theological lesson that this desperate generation will listen to; and for that reason I will learn to laugh again, and more heartily and humbly than ever before. Then, and only then, I think, will I be able to get through to the likes of Jonathon, who is so fundamentally and deeply sad, and show him a type of joy that he has never known or believed to be true.

Unless we learn the joy and the hope of our faith and express it through laughter, then, I believe, we are good for nothing and no different from anybody else.

THERE'S A SIXTEEN-YEAR-OLD GIRL IN ME SOMEWHERE. SHE'S IN THERE, POUNDING A FIST ON MY ORGANS AND SCREAMING, "YOU ARE NOT IMPORTANT!" AND, "NOBODY LOVES YOU ENOUGH!" WHEN WILL I BE RID OF HER?

FIRST FRIDAY IN LENT

by Jessica Griffith

Tuesday night I talked to my sister for about an hour while she watched *Queer Eye for the Straight Guy* and only half listened to me. She called to tell me that Tim can't come to the wedding because he has to work. They are switching operating systems at the plant, so there will be no vacation time in October.

I—meaning the twenty-seven-year-old me who is logical and mature and not even that excited about showing up for this wedding myself because I can't stand the thought of everyone looking at me for so long and am sure I will trip while walking down the aisle—is not really upset by this. But there's a sixteen-year-old girl in me somewhere telling me that I should be. She's still in there. She's in there, pounding a fist on my organs and screaming, "You are not important!" and, "Nobody loves you enough!" She's the one who still gets drunk and smokes cigarettes and approaches everything with selfish entitlement. She is not a very good person. She's a teenager. When will I be rid of her?

She snuck out on Wednesday night, too. Dave and I were having a perfectly nice night. It was Ash Wednesday and we'd gone to the 7 p.m. Mass at Sacred Heart and had the ashes ground into our foreheads. My favorite priest gave me my ashes. He always strikes me as the kind of guy who could have gone one of two ways: the priesthood or the stage. He reminds me of a character in a Tim Burton movie. Specifically, he reminds me of Bill Murray in *Ed Wood*. He has a great sweep of silver hair and he is vaguely effeminate and very dramatic. He really attacked my forehead with the ashes, booming "Remember! You are dust, and to dust you will return!" as if he were the very voice of God. He gripped my skull with his fingers and made the Sign of the Cross between my eyes with his thumb. These were not the dusty gray ashes like they used to give at the church of my childhood. These were dark like coal and full of pebbles that felt like ground-up bones. I felt my eyes widen with a combination of shock and ecstasy. Yes! I wanted to shout. This is why I love Catholicism! I swear he smiled a little at my reaction. We had our own thing going on up there. I considered wiping the ashes off and going back through the line.

The feeling I got from that priest's strong hand on my forehead and his deep voice professing my mortality stayed with me while Dave and I went home and heated up lasagna from Whole Foods and opened the bottle of wine from the woman he'd helped when she fell on our street. But after this especially gratifying Mass nothing

Jessica Griffith

on TV was dramatic enough for us. We settled on *South Park* because it was the one where all the boys—except Kyle, the lonely Jew—are preparing to make their first communions and first confessions. Each is overcome by his sins. They become obsessed with making confessions. They are lined up outside the confessional, demanding forgiveness, when they throw open the door and catch the priest buggering some woman. There's a side plot about Satan, whom the illustrators depict as a giant red bull dressed like a professional wrestler. He is dating a milquetoast guy who eats organic and tries to understand Satan's feelings for his ex, Saddam Hussein. This episode is the first of two, and it ends with a cliffhanger. Will Satan dump his new man and return to Saddam? Will the newly zealous South Park youth, led by a proselytizing Cartman, reform Catholicism? Dave and I were having great fun. We finished a little more than half the bottle of wine and split a package of Fig Newtons for dessert.

Then Dave started talking about his novel again, and he's really excited about it right now because he finally feels that he has found the way to tell this story so that it is moral and not merely self-indulgent, not just a sex, drugs, and rock and roll story, as the multicultural women of the English department like to call the stories by the young white guys. But I know that Dave is really writing the stories of all his important and formative relationships—aren't we all?—and the sixteen-year-old suddenly wanted to know where she fit on this continuum.

We love each other. Of course. My grown-up self is sure of it. I have never before felt the psychic closeness that I feel with Dave. With his patience and his goodness—and yes, I swear, he is essentially good in a way that I've never known anyone else to be—he is easing me into adulthood, even though I was so sure that I was the one leading him. But love and marriage kind of snuck up on us. I thought we were just fooling around. This was the first relationship that I ever entered with every intention of ending it after the first night. I was looking for a fling, and it shows me now just how close to spiritual bankruptcy I was that this seemed like the best thing I could do for myself, emotionally and professionally. Yes, we were attracted to each other, and yes, I remember the very first time I saw him getting coffee at the Starbucks in the basement of the Cathedral of Learning and I felt that inner switch flip. But it was just that, a switch. Not a blown transformer. And this is where the sixteen-year-old comes in, with her manic-panicked hair and her nose ring and her homemade tattoo and the cigarette in her mouth. She won't be ignored.

Where is my great love story? she demands. Dave doesn't know how to deal with this little girl.

Don't ask me to explain it, he told me. I love you like I never knew I could love anyone, he said. And the cliché made him angry. And I mistook his anger at the cliché for anger at me and before I knew it we were facing opposite directions in our bed and drifting off to sleep in silence.

We both woke at the same time about an hour later. Conan O'Brien was on, and they were doing my favorite bit, where they project some famous person's head on a

TV screen next to Conan's desk, and an actor moves his lips in the famous person's head and impersonates him or her—poorly. It's so low-tech, it reminds me of something Jennifer and I would have done when we were little girls. It's totally hilarious. On this night they were doing Arnold Schwarzenegger, and when I woke up Schwarzenegger was yelling at Conan, "THAT'S GUVENA SCHWARZANAYGA TO YOU, CO-NAN!!" And I couldn't help myself from laughing out loud. Hilarious, I tell you.

So then Dave was laughing at me for laughing at this, and then he was curled up at my side with his head on my shoulder, and I moved my fingers in the curls at the nape of his neck, the curls that mean he needs a haircut, and I felt sorry, because now that I'd slept off a little of that red wine and Newtons I know that he was only frustrated because he couldn't think of the right words to talk about love and that he was probably disappointed that I would want him to. It's little moments like this that make me feel so petty and immature and ashamed and filled with admiration for him, and so grateful that despite my constantly sticking my head deep into the dark cavity of the proverbial horse's mouth, God continues to bless me.

I take it back. I do remember a moment when the transformer blew. It was the day after our first night together, and we were lying head-to-toe on my sofa nursing hangovers, passing a pint of peanut butter cup ice cream back and forth and watching *The Exorcist* on cable.

"You know what my favorite part is?" Dave asked, and passed the pint. "It's when the priest says that the devil wants us to despair."

And that's when I felt my stomach get all hot and tingly, and I said, yes. "Yes! That's my favorite part, too."

Thursday night Rachael and I went to Pittsburgh Jeans Company and the salesgirls were unbelievably rude to us and implied that Rachael was too big to wear fashionable jeans. All she wanted was a pair of jeans that don't show her crack when she sits down, and these girls kept yelling over the loud techno *unz-unz-unz* that it wouldn't matter because she would only wear these jeans "out" which I guess means "to the club," where she wouldn't be sitting down anyway. I thought Rachael would flip. So this is where the women's movement has gotten us, I could almost hear her thinking. They basically kicked us out of the place, and now I wish that I had gone back and banged on the glass door and flipped them both off. When I got home, it was about 8 p.m. and Dave still wasn't there. All the lights were off except the dim yellow lamp in the corner of the living room. We never turn that one off.

It's been so long since I have come home to an empty house. I am instantly worried. Usually Dave calls me at least once every afternoon. He calls me at my office from the office he shares with the other adjuncts at the university. He talks so softly that I am always asking him to repeat himself, or speak up. He very rarely has anything to say. He is just calling because he can. Sometimes he reads me a paragraph or two of something he has written or something that he is reading. Or he tells me that he has band practice. Or he asks for a ride from Oakland. Or he asks me if I need a ride home, if he's taken the car. He

lingers on the phone. This makes me impatient. I'm trying to work, which is hard enough when you share a one-
room office with three or four women you adore, and
when you hate the phone anyway and can't wait to get
off.

But I've had a yucky feeling all evening because I didn't
get one of those calls today, and now this house is empty
except for that awful yellow light. Where is he? The car is
parked on the street behind Kate's Volvo, where it is
always parked. We walk or take the bus everywhere
because we never pay our parking tickets. The keys are in
the mailbox as usual, hidden in plain view.

I struggle to remember the morning. Dave leaves so
early to catch the bus to make his 8 a.m. class that it is
still dark out. He comes into the bedroom smelling like
soap and Speedstick deodorant, the curly ends of his hair
still wet, and he leans over the bed and kisses me goodbye. When he kissed me this morning, did he say he'd be
late? I can't remember. Damn.

I have a deadline the next day, but I'm too worried to
write. I've been fighting worry all evening, and in fact was
proud that I didn't mention it once to Rachael, but now
it's approaching full boil and about to blow my lid off.

I turn on the TV and see that *Twin Peaks: Fire Walk
With Me* is on IFC. I pick it up about half way, when
Laura Palmer is just beginning to suspect that her dad
may be a shady character. She is in her bedroom, and she
is preoccupied by two framed paintings. One is obviously creepy: It is just a cracked door in a dark hallway. The
other is kitschy, but creepy. In it, a family or maybe a

group of children gather at a table, and an angel stands at the head keeping watch. While Laura watches, the angel disappears from the picture. This is when things really start to go haywire.

I really shouldn't be watching this right now because I am already so jumpy and so worried and looking out the window every thirty seconds, hoping I hear a car. But Dave and I have been watching all the *Twin Peaks* episodes on DVD lately, and I haven't seen this prequel since I was in college, and I am marveling at how obvious and heavy-handed it all seems, when I used to think it was so cryptic and cool. Sometimes I underestimate how much I have grown up, and revisiting the things I loved at nineteen and twenty is such a great reminder. It's also helpful to read the margin comments from all the books I thought I understood. Those make me blush. I was so sure that I had everything figured out. And now, with every year, every passing day, I become less so. Can I really call that maturity? It feels like going backward. Every so often I check the phone to be sure it is plugged in, and that I haven't missed a message. Where is he?

I am telling myself that he is fine, remembering that he always has band practice on Thursday nights. He will be home any minute. But there she is with her shrill, hysterical voice, a Mickey's Big Mouth Lager in one hand and a Camel Light in the other. "He's never coming home!" she shouts. She is always shouting this.

"He's gone! And your last memory of him is fuzzy and half-lit and mostly olfactory and now you will always cry when you smell Speedstick Classic Clean and Head and

Shoulders!" She is almost happy because she loves nothing more than being right.

I try to smother her. Come on, I say out loud. Grow up! I command her/me. Because I/we are grown up enough to watch this corny movie alone at night and not worry about Dave, who is just fine, who is probably having a great time smoking a joint and playing his trombone in downtown Pittsburgh. You/I have to get over this idea that every time we say goodbye it will be our last. It is making me crazy. And it makes him crazy, the way I am always saying, "Please be careful." I say it a lot. I say it with eyes wide and hands gripping the sides of his arms. Not just when he's going out of town for the weekend with his band to play a show, or to go to an old friend's wedding. I do it even if he is just running out to get a newspaper, or to pick up another six-pack for a party we're having.

It's almost worse then—and this is her talking again—because wouldn't it be awful to think I lost him for a Sunday edition of the *New York Times*? For one more Dos Equis with a lime? She tells me it would haunt me for the rest of my life, that I let him leave without one last important moment where we looked each other in the eye. I have to perform this superstitious little ceremony where I say the right words and touch him the right way, as if I am blessing him. As if this warning or this appeal—"Please be careful"—followed by this charm—"I love you"—will protect him. He humors me/us. But he doesn't know that sometimes I make the Sign of the Cross over the car before he goes. He caught me doing that before I got on a plane once, and he laughed and teased me for so long that I have to do this furtively now, on the sly, when I hope he's not looking.

I think he humors me because he knows this story: The first time my mom ever left me home alone, she left me at home to go to the grocery store. I must have been eleven or twelve because I begged her to leave me, so I could feel like a teenager. I was sure I'd be fine, and I was, for about an hour. I played my records on my dad's forbidden stereo and danced in the living room. But when she left it was afternoon; soon it would be getting dark, and she still wasn't back. I started to feel sick that I had insisted that she go alone. I would be forever responsible for what happened to her, and I was suddenly sure she was dead. I felt certain that there had been an accident. By the time she pulled up in the driveway I was sitting on our front porch, on the bench with the heart cut out of the back. I was hysterical, crying and sweaty and snotty. It turned out that she had gone to Hancock Fabrics to buy Jennifer and me some more yarn for the friendship bracelets we were into making back then. I was so mad at her for scaring me that I never made another bracelet again, and every time I saw the yarn in the little yellow plastic bag I felt sick, the way I would feel when she told us she had cancer, the same lurching feeling, like vertigo.

Dave knows this story and he is so good and so patient, and so we always say, "I love you," even if we are only parting for a few minutes. We call it to each other from upstairs to downstairs. While he is leaning over me, smelling like deodorant and soap and the only light is from the bathroom, still steamy from his shower. Even if he has just called to tell me that he has band practice, or to ask me how many eggs to use in a recipe, we say, "I love you" before we hang up.

These are the same sorts of compulsions that made me crazy as a kid. These are the same things that made me think, when my mom really did die, that I had always had a sixth sense about it. That I had always known it would happen. But how psychic is that? Of course we know that everyone will die one day, that it is just a matter of time until the day that someone leaves and doesn't come home. There's nothing so intuitive about that. It didn't even happen the way I thought it would. She wasn't yanked from me by a trip to the grocery store. She faded in a long, torturous illness; it took a year.

What was so different about me, I guess, was not the revelation at all but the obsession with the revelation. Was/am I the only person in the world who was aware that we are all dying? Clearly, I was/am not. So how did/do other people ignore it? How can we do anything or say anything that distracts us from certain mortality? How can we say goodbye for even a few minutes when we know that WE ARE ALL GOING TO DIE? That one day it really will be our last goodbye?

Just as the angel appears to Laura in that red room with that black and white op-art floor, I hear his keys in the lock.

"You are NOT watching *Twin Peaks!*" he says, disbelieving, depositing his trombone at the foot of the stairs. He knows me well enough but he is still sometimes shocked by the million and one ways I choose to horrify myself every day. It turns out he did tell me that he had practice tonight, and that I didn't remember. He told me this morning when he came in the bedroom to tell me goodbye and that he loved me before he rushed out to catch the bus on the corner of Dallas Avenue in the dark. I was still pretty much asleep.

And so he's here and the anxiety fades, like the angel in Laura Palmer's picture. It's not the sort of relief you'd think it is. It's a grudging relief. The sixteen-year-old is retreating, but she's still scowling with her arms crossed over her chest, and saying so what? So we're okay for now. This was just a rehearsal—only a hint of what it will feel like when he really doesn't come home. The sixteen-year-old wants to stay mad. I shut her up because he tells me he had a rough day.

He tells me that he had a rough day, a departmental meeting about how to teach "difficult" stories, that ended up, as it always does, to be all about race. Our English department wants to teach morality through multiculturalism. Dave says I would have been proud, because he stood up and asked what kind of system or standard they were using for the basis of this morality. He is turning into the C. S. Lewis of Pitt. And he's not even that religious, and when he is, he's so private about it. But he is white, and male, and I sense him casting about for a valid academic identity—a way to distinguish himself. Nobody ever talks about God, he tells me. Nobody ever mentions religion, much less Christianity. Instead we are supposed to know what is right and what is wrong simply by empathy. We feel bad that a man was lynched. We recognize that this behavior is wrong. That racism is wrong. But why?

I don't know what came over me, he says as he flings his scarf over the coat rack and kicks off his shoes. I must have been filled with the Holy Spirit or something. But I just couldn't take it anymore. Check this out, he says, and he shuffles through his bag for a stapled handout. "Stages of Moral Development" is printed in bold and centered at the top of the page. Stapled to this is an excerpt from "Teaching/Learning Anti-Racism: Stages of White Identity Development." According to the logic of this handout, the highest stage of moral development a white person can attain is when he or she (a) "replaces conformity to racism with a world view that affirms the value of all people and cultures, and seeks to share power and resources" and (b) when he or she "has learned how to function in multiracial groups, learned how to take responsibility for racism, and is comfortable examining one's own participation in racist systems."

"Is this a joke?" I ask him, and he throws his hands up and goes to the kitchen to get a beer.

I am in awe of this handout, of the earnestness in it. Someone, everyone believes this? I think I must not understand. I must be missing something. I must be mis-understanding, misquoting, taking it all out of context. This is the secret to being a good person, to having a valuable contribution to society, to history, to academia, to literature? This is the key to good writing, good teach-ing? Multiculturalism?

I think—my dad was right. This is all completely soulless—these careers we have chosen, this lofty tenure to which we aspire. Professors flush dark with embarrassment or anger or impatience when you mention God. Or they look at you blankly, or with pity.

This is one of those things that amazes me. How, when we all know for sure that we will all one day die, can we type a handout that tells us the way to a fully realized life is through awareness of racism? Even if you're an atheist. Don't these people know we are all going into the ground one day, each of us?

How can I even waste my time and energy holding this piece of paper when my heart might stop while I'm reading it?

On Friday afternoon I go to the Stations of the Cross at Sacred Heart, and this is what happens.

The kids file in behind their teachers, and I see "me" at every age. Quiet and intimidated in second grade, checking out the big kids with curiosity. Whispering to my girlfriends in fifth grade, already growing so fast, taller than all the other kids and slouched over trying to hide it. Me in seventh grade, trying to sit next to the boy that I like.

By eighth grade all the girls are taller than the boys, and their plaid skirts are getting too small, and their feet are too big on their skinny legs. They wear lip gloss and earrings. The boys are getting acne and greasy hair. I recognize all of them. But really it's hard to tell their ages, especially the younger ones. Those distinctions seemed so rigid when I was there. The leap from second to third grade was big and dangerous.

The church is overwhelmed by the scent of these kids. The smaller ones smell like sweat, like recess. Anne Lamott wrote that she thinks this is what God must smell like, like the skin behind a little kid's ear. Like unwashed potatoes. The older girls smell like melon lip gloss and gum and perfume, but still, despite it all, they smell faintly like sweat and recess. They are eyeing me with suspicion, my sweatshirt and jeans. I think I should spit out my gum and set a good example. But I feel like I could put on my uniform and walk back to class with them in single file and still feel so needy and awkward, so determined to talk out of turn, to get some air time. Sometimes the girl in me isn't even sixteen. Sometimes she's thirteen.

Maybe I've overestimated her and she's always thirteen, the age I was when my mom got cancer. Maybe she's eleven, the age I was when she was late coming home because she bought that yarn.

Once they are all settled in the pews, one of their teachers stands in the front of the church and calls them to attention by saying, "let's practice." And then she hums the refrain you sing between the stations, the *Stabat Mater*.

The three lines change with every verse, but the tune is the same. It has the simplicity of a nursery rhyme; it is see-sawy, up-downy, sing-songy, easy for a young shaky voice to master, but it is all in minor key and so sad. I haven't been to Stations of the Cross in fifteen years, and when their young voices started I suddenly drowned in nostalgia. The tune and all those little voices hit me like a wave can hit you when you're unprepared, when you're not ready to dive in and ride it. It knocks the breath out of you, and leaves you on your ass on the beach with seaweed in your hair and sand in your bikini, not knowing up from down; manhandled by a force stronger than a man, feeling a little foolish at your own weakness.

"Jesus, Lord, condemned, defiled

May we too be meek and mild

As we tread your holy way."

My throat constricted and I choked on a sob. Two of the big kids, I'm guessing seventh or eighth graders because the girl is wearing lip gloss, read the text for the stations. They flank the priest in front of the altar. They probably rotate every week, or maybe only the best readers get this honor. That was how it happened in my Catholic school. These kids are good readers, even if they sound more like they should be reading aloud from *Seventeen* magazine than from the Passion. How can a twelve-year-old wring the right kind of painful humility from Psalm 118?

"I lie prostrate in the dust; give me life according to your word.

I declared my ways, and you answered me; teach me your commands.

Make me understand the way of your precepts, and I will meditate on your wondrous deeds."

I wonder what this little girl is thinking as she reads these words from her little *Way of the Cross* booklet, with the cartoons of Jesus in his long white robe. Is she worried about her hair? Her math grade? If her crush is watching? Or is she really praying?

Or is it a little of all of those things? Is she worried that her prayers are futile?

"My soul weeps for sorrow, strengthen me with your words."

I am in tears. I often am.

Hearing all these young voices enunciating scripture in unison—sloppy unison, but still unison!—to hear this again is to remember a feeling that I have long forgotten . . . a feeling that is something like home and a little tribal. It is a feeling of connectedness with the living and the dead, with nature and super-nature. And in this moment it is enough to convince me that my children will go to Catholic school, despite all the guilt of the flesh and even the comparatively bad education. Because this is why I'm a writer, isn't it? This is why I see symbols and metaphors and poetry and death everywhere. Because of the rhythm of these words, these heads all dipping in unison, the bending of knees to kneelers, the tiny sad voices singing the *Stabat Mater*.

Or maybe I should be in Catholic school now. Maybe this is the vocation I feel I can barely hear. To be the one who stands up and says, "Let's practice."

But I barely have enough time to digest the prayers and the Passion and the intensity of my nostalgia and how much I miss my Catholic school and the life I had when I was this reading girl's age, with a mom and a dad and everything in the right place, before we are on the fourteenth station, Jesus is Laid in the Tomb, and it is all over.

The stations have flown by—nothing like I remember. I remember these fourteen sections, the twelve hours from Gethsemane to Calvary, taking a little eternity. You do the Stations of the Cross during the last part of a Friday afternoon, the last bit of the school day before going home with a friend or to a slumber party, or to a Lenten fish dinner with my parents and grandparents at Thonn's Restaurant on Pontchartrain Drive. It is painful—so much kneeling and standing and kneeling and standing—and boring, and because it is painful and boring, it is considered a penance, for which you earn a plenary indulgence from the Church—an earned bit of grace, a blessing. But this Passion is over in forty-five minutes. It has barely begun when it's over and all the little ones are hop-scotching from brick to brick all the way down the center aisle and out the double doors.

I have to wait a minute with my head hung low, dabbing at my eyes while the big kids single-file out, teachers shushing them as they whisper and giggle in ears. When I emerge the little ones are standing on the steps in the three o'clock sun, waiting for their rides. The older girls are lying in the grass with their plaid uniform skirts hiked up and their knee socks rolled around their ankles.

While I walk home I think again of that girl in me, and how sometimes I love her. I want to hug her and brush her hair and paint her nails. Maybe I don't want her to go. Maybe she stays because I insist on it. She is, after all, what remains.

Priest: We adore you oh Christ, and we bless you.
GENUFLECT.

All: Because by your holy cross, you have redeemed the world.

The rhythm of the stations is still in my head. It is the first Friday of Lent, and Dave is going to play a show in Detroit. We have a craving for fried seafood, so we meet for oysters in Market Square before saying "I love you" and "goodbye" on the corner of Fifth Avenue.

I/we make the Sign of the Cross over the car that will bring him back to us tomorrow, safe.

THE GLITTERING PRIZES OF SECU-
LARISM ARE VANITY, AS IS LIFE
ITSELF WITHOUT ITS EXTENSION
INTO ETERNITY. ON THE OTHER
HAND, THE MOST HUMBLE LIFE
WHEN SEEN UNDER THE ASPECT
OF ETERNITY IS INVESTED WITH AN
UNIMAGINABLE GLORY.

ETERNITY IN THE HERE AND NOW

by Harold Fickett

If I suddenly felt that this life is all there is, I'm not sure what I would do. Rage would enter into it, I'm sure—the rage that drives so many people to shatter their own lives and the lives of those around them.

Because I am a person of faith, I remain open to my faith being disproved. Let's say the bones of Jesus were exhumed tomorrow, and the world learned that the bodily resurrection of Jesus was a hoax. How would I react?

I would not make an easy transition into a "spiritualized" understanding of Jesus' life and mission—an ethics of universal brotherhood looking toward a utopian horizon. Not at all. Losing faith would destroy the fundamental premise of my life. Everything I've lived for, taught my children, and written about would be nullified.

But the loss of my way of being in the world would be the least of it. What I would most dread, as I've considered such a nightmare, would be a cosmic claustrophobia, as the whole world became a coffin with the lid descending. At first, I would probably quake with fear, and then experience the unstoppable rage of our times.

Why should any creature possess consciousness of mortality and longings for the immortal if these served, at best, an obscure socio-biological agenda? That's not a bad joke or even a dark one—that's night itself.

As I look back over my life, and particularly the last twenty years as a Catholic, I have always known the deep and ultimate pleasure of eternity. It's not that I have been comforted by the thought of future rewards compensating for present difficulties. This hasn't entered into it at all.

Rather, my soul has luxuriated in the knowledge that each aspect of my life has an ultimate significance. That in God's redemption of fallen creation, all that I have known, given, failed to give, miscarried, or completed will be taken up into a final reconciliation that will purge away the dross and leave God's will as all in all.

In the Catholic scheme of things, the thousand memories that flood our minds will all, everyone, be taken into this final reckoning. Even the quiet moment with my seven-year-old daughter Eve, when she said, "I find that really disturbing," and I got a big kick out of her imitating my love of hyperbole. The moment when I touched my father's forehead in his coffin and found it even colder than I had imagined. The night I drove home, quite drunk, from a party with graduate school friends through a heavy snowstorm and could only see ahead of me by sticking my head out the window, not having the sense, in my inebriation, to wait for the car to warm and the windows to clear of their coating of frozen rain. The day a publisher spiked a book I had worked on for two years. The moment when I saw love in the eyes of my future wife that was so deep I knew this lovely young woman wanted to have children with me.

If this life is all there is, these things would be passing shadows, flickerings of electro-chemical responses, or as the Bible puts it, sounding brass and tinkling cymbals. They would not be the marks on my soul of the good and evil I have known, with enduring implications.

I remember going from my Christian elementary school into a public junior high. The usual things were wrong with that junior high, but beyond all that, I remember how the atmosphere seemed thin—a dampened and flattened melody. The notes being struck in that secular context never rang true—as if someone were trying to play a vibraphone covered with a cloth. *Plink, plink, plink, plink.*

We were supposed to get a good education . . . so we could be good citizens . . . so we could make a good living . . . so we could be respected, even celebrated, in the future. Even at twelve and thirteen, I couldn't help thinking, Who cares?

Chesterton said that the individual is more important than any temporal institution because the individual has an eternal destiny, while the greatest of civilizations are passing phenomena. This understanding, which lies at the heart of Christianity, gives to each life and every experience in that life an immeasurable dignity.

We are playing not merely for keeps but for ever.

Dostoevsky's character Ivan Karamazov believed that if God is dead, "everything is lawful." Or, as Flannery O'Connor's Misfit put it,

> Jesus was the only One that ever raised the dead . . . and He shouldn't have done it. He thrown everything off balance. If He did what He said, then it's nothing for you to do but throw away everything and follow Him, and if He didn't, then it's nothing for you to do but enjoy the few minutes you got left the best way you can—by killing somebody or burning down his house or doing some other meanness to him. No pleasure but meanness.

For myself, being of a craven temperament, I think I would just get permanently drunk.

The glittering prizes of secularism are vanity, as is life itself without its extension into eternity. On the other hand, the most humble life when seen under the aspect of eternity is invested with an unimaginable glory. To live possessed by this hope provides a strength that transcends every circumstance.

I keep betting my life that Christianity is true.

ABOUT THE CONTRIBUTORS

BRIAN **PESSARO** writes on Catholic life and spirituality from Tallahassee, Florida, where he lives with his wife and two children.

ELIZABETH **WIRTH** is the former managing editor of *Re:Generation Quarterly*. A freelance writer and full-time mother, she lives in Massachusetts with her husband, Karl, and their three children.

PATRICK **STILL** writes occasionally on Catholic topics. He lives in the Midwest, somewhere along the Mississippi River.

ANNA **BROADWAY** holds an M.A. in religious studies and is the author of the forthcoming memoir *Sexless in the City* (Random House, 2008), based on her blog of the same name. Her writing has appeared in *Beliefnet*, *Radiant*, *Paste*, *Relevant*, and other print and web publications. She lives near San Francisco, California, and is the only non-Catholic contributor in the book. She is a Presbyterian.

DAVID **MORRISON** is a reporter and writer based in the Washington, DC, area. A former gay activist, he is the author of *Beyond Gay* (OSV, 1999). In addition to writing and speaking on Christian discipleship, chastity, and same-sex attraction, Morrison has reported on topics such as aquaculture, international trade, financial regulation, and human rights. He is also the founder of Courage Online, a moderated support community of people living with same-sex attraction. A convert to Catholicism, David is the godfather to two beautiful children in Northern Virginia.

JESSICA **GRIFFITH** has written for *Elle, Crisis, Notre Dame Magazine, Image, Creative Nonfiction,* and many other publications. She received her M.F.A. in creative writing from the University of Pittsburgh. She lives in southern Virginia with her husband David and her daughter Charlotte.

PAULA **HUSTON** is currently working on a book about forgiveness for Paraclete Press. She is the author of *By Way of Grace: Moving from Faithfulness to Holiness* and *The Holy Way: Practices for a Simple Life* (Loyola Press). She is also the co-editor of *Signatures of Grace: Catholic Writers on the Sacraments.* Her website is www.PaulaHuston.com.

MATTHEW **LICKONA** writes regularly on assorted subjects for the the *San Diego Reader,* a weekly newspaper, and is the author of *Swimming with Scapulars: True Confessions of a Young Catholic* (Loyola Press). He is a graduate of Thomas Aquinas College and lives in La Mesa, California, with his wife Deirdre and their five children.

LISA **LICKONA** writes on theology and spirituality for Catholic publications. She holds a master's degree and a licentiate from the John Paul II Institute for Studies on Marriage and Family, and lives in McGraw, New York, with her husband Mark and their six children.

REBECCA **ROBINSON** writes from Richmond, Virginia, where she explores the line between truth and fiction and awaits the birth of her first child.

EVE **TUSHNET** is a freelance writer in Washington, DC. She was received into the Catholic Church in 1998. She has written for *Commonweal*, the *National Catholic Register*, the *New York Post*, and other publications. She blogs on religious and cultural topics and assorted randomness at www.eve-tushnet.blogspot.com.

JOHN **ZMIRAK** is the author of *The Bad Catholic's Guide to Good Living*, and *The Bad Catholic's Guide to Wine, Whiskey & Song* (Crossroad Publishing). His writing has appeared in *USA Today*, *Investor's Business Daily*, *Commonweal*, *The Weekly Standard*, the *New Republic*, *The Atlantic Monthly*, *The American Conservative*, the *National Catholic Register*, and *First Things*. He is currently Writer-in-Residence at Thomas More College of the Liberal Arts in Merrimack, New Hampshire.

JACK **SMITH** is editor of *The Catholic Key*, newspaper of the Diocese of Kansas City-St. Joseph. He is former editor of *Catholic San Francisco*.

MARION **MAENDEL** was raised at the Bruderhof, now known as Church Communities International. After several years with the Houston Catholic Worker, she studied classical philosophy and theology with the monks of the Brothers of St. John in Laredo, Texas. During her year and a half stay there, she was baptized into the Catholic Church. She lives in Houston with her husband, Andres, and their son, Dominic.

AUSTEN **IVEREIGH** is a journalist whose writing has appeared in the *Guardian*, the *Spectator*, and numerous other publications. He was coordinator for the *Da Vinci Code* Response Group and the Strangers into Citizens campaign, in England. He is former deputy editor of the Catholic weekly, *The Tablet*, and former director for Public Affairs of the Archbishop of Westminster, Cardinal Cormac Murphy-O'Connor.

JOHN **JALSEVAC** recently graduated from Christendom College in Virginia with a B.A. in philosophy and a minor in theology. He was editor of his college journal, *The Rambler*, and has written and professionally published hundreds of articles, mostly for *LifeSiteNews*, where he served as an assistant editor. He is planning on pursuing his doctorate in clinical psychology.

HAROLD **FICKETT** is the author of novels, biographies, and works of spirituality, including *The Holy Fool, The Living Christ,* and *Dancing with the Divine.* He was a co-founder of the journal *Image,* and has collaborated with Charles Colson on several books, including *The Faith* and *The Good Life.*

ACKNOWLEDGMENTS

So many great people have contributed to the making of Godspy.com, and this book. If only it were possible to thank them all here. I hope and pray that they know how deeply grateful I am for their help and support.

Without the encouragement and fine work of Tom Grady and his staff at Ave Maria Press, this book would not have happened.

I want to express my gratitude to two spiritual masters who have guided me. Fr. Benedict Groeschel introduced me to Christian spirituality, and his advice helped me understand how God draws straight with crooked lines. Msgr. Lorenzo Albacete's theological insights opened my eyes to "the mystery" of Christ. His daring presence within secular culture has been a model for GodSpy from the start. I have relied heavily on the wisdom, witness, and wit of these two men.

GodSpy would not have been possible without the support and friendship of Harold Fickett, Austen

Ivereigh, and David Scott, three of the finest Catholic editors and writers, or without the diligent daily work and support of Lori Chaplin, the site's managing editor.

Only the encouragement and love of my family—my wife Anna and my sons, Gianni and Thomas—has made it possible to take on the difficult and risky business of publishing GodSpy.

Lastly, I'd like to thank Fr. Paul Murray, O.P., for inspiring the name GodSpy, which comes from his article on Shakespeare's religious vision, published in the journal *Communio*. There he quotes King Lear, at the end of the eponymous play, as he invites his daughter Cordelia to join him as they "take upon 's the mystery of things, / As if we were God's spies."

Editor ANGELO **MATERA** is the publisher of the online Catholic magazine, godspy.com, and writes frequently about social justice, war, and the economy for Catholic publications. He is also a publishing and marketing consultant with twenty-five years experience working with secular media companies such as Time Inc. and *Forbes Magazine*. His recent projects include the launches of *Faith & Family Magazine* and *The American Conservative*. Matera is also the former CEO of Circle Media, publisher of *The National Catholic Register*.

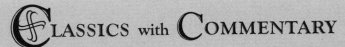

CLASSICS with COMMENTARY

Classics with Commentary, a series in the Christian Classics line devoted to rediscovering classic Christian literature, mines the depths of the rich tradition of Christian spirituality. Critical translations accompanied by timely and accessible commentary and probing questions revitalize these works for another generation of spiritual pilgrims.

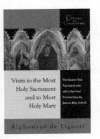

Visits to the Most Holy Sacrament and to Most Holy Mary

Alphonsus de Liguori
The Classic Text Translated and with a Spiritual Commentary
Dennis Billy, C.Ss.R.

The first complete and faithful English translation from its original Italian o
Visits to the Most Holy Sacrament and to Most Holy Mary, a devotional classic b
St. Alphonsus de Liguori.

ISBN: 9780870612442 / 160 pages / $15.95

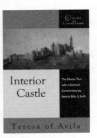

Interior Castle

Teresa of Avila
The Classic Text with a Spiritual Commentary
Dennis Billy, C.Ss.R.

The classic E. Allison Peers translation of this Christian favorite is united with fres
spiritual commentary, making it the only edition of Teresa of Avila's classic to remai
faithful to her mystical vision while providing spiritual nourishment.

ISBN: 9780870612411 / 320 pages / $16.95

The Imitation of Christ

Thomas À Kempis
A Spiritual Commentary and Reader's Guide
Dennis Billy, C.Ss.R.

Fr. Billy highlights how today's Christians can interpret and apply *The Imitation* t
their own spiritual journeys with the help of William Creasy's accessible translatio
Billy opens each chapter with a brief introduction and completes each one wit
reflection questions to help readers apply the text to their lives.

ISBN: 9780870612343 / 272 pages / $15.95

COMING
FALL 2008

Spiritual Friendship

Aelred of Rievaulx
The Classic Text with a Spiritual Commentary
Dennis Billy, C.Ss.R.

Available from your bookstore or from
ave maria press / Notre Dame, IN 46556
www.avemariapress.com / Ph: 800-282-1865
A Ministry of the Indiana Province of Holy Cross

Keycode: FD912070000